A history of printed textiles

A history of
PRINTED TEXTILES

BLOCK · ROLLER · SCREEN
DESIGN · DYES · FIBRES · DISCHARGE · RESIST
FURTHER SOURCES FOR RESEARCH

Stuart Robinson

Studio Vista London

To S.

'All living things yearn for colour.' GOETHE

'. . . I, to Cornhill; after some trials I bought for my wife a chintz . . . to decorate her new boudoir, which is very nice.' PEPYS

'. . . We graciously will and decree herewith, in earnest, that . . . on this side of the Oder and Elbe and beyond . . . neither painted nor printed calicos . . . are allowed to be worn by anybody . . .' KING FREDERICK WILLIAM I OF PRUSSIA, 1721

'PRAY be careful to keep the Book clean, the Patterns have cost a deal of Money, and are easily Spoiled by children, or Careless Persons putting their hands on them; it is therefore hoped and entreated, that the utmost care will be taken to sully the Patterns as little as possible, and when any Lady sends for a Sight of the Book it is entreated she will give Orders that it be Returned immediately.' *From a bound sample book, Carlisle,* 1780–5

'Birds 10d a yard Talwin & Foster.' 1770

'To my daughter, my bed, window curtain and chairs with the covers of Mr Jones's printing.' *From the will of a cotton printer of Mitcham,* 1790

'Enter love, disguised as a maker of pictured cloths.'—'Love is Enough.' WILLIAM MORRIS

'We should have nothing in our houses which we did not either know to be useful or believe to be beautiful.' WILLIAM MORRIS, *c.* 1870

© Stuart Robinson
First published in Great Britain 1969
by Studio Vista Limited, Blue Star House,
Highgate Hill, London N19
Set in 11 on 12 pt Baskerville

Printed in Great Britain
by W & J Mackay & Co Ltd, Chatham

SBN 289 79761 6

Contents

Preface

This book is intended both as an outline history of printed textiles and as a comprehensive source book for the further study of this topic. My experience over a number of years in advising students preparing special studies upon decorated textiles has shown me how scattered is the necessary information in a wide variety of articles, journals and books, many of which are now out of print. As far as I know this, and its companion volume dealing with dyed textiles, are the first books to cover the subject in detail.

I am greatly indebted to a number of authorities and researchers in this field and would particularly express my appreciation of the advice and practical assistance given me by the following: Dr P. Quensel and S. Napier, Editors *CIBA Review*, for their unfailing courtesy, the loan of a number of illustration originals, and permission to quote from the *Review*; P. R. Schwartz, President of the Musée de L'Impression sur Etoffes, Mulhouse, Alsace; the staff of the Victoria and Albert Museum and in particular Natalie Rothstein, Assistant Keeper of the Department of Textiles, and her colleagues Wendy Hefford and Edmund Capon, A. G. Mitchell and Veronica Murphy of the Indian Section and Barbara Morris of the Circulation Department; B. A. L. Cranstone, Assistant Keeper, Department of Ethnography and Paul Snelgrove, Department of Prints and Drawings, both of the British Museum; Professor Roger Nicholson of the School of Textile Design, Royal College of Art, London; Nicholas Sutton of *Design Magazine*; J. F. Turner, Dyestuffs Division, I.C.I., Manchester and W. J. Houlding, Richard Bett and June Kenyon of Arthur Sanderson and Sons Ltd.

I would also place on record my gratitude to my colleagues Norman Furlong for his advice in the writing of the text, Muriel Somerfield for much of the photography, and my wife, Patricia, without whose unfailing encouragement, proof-reading and advice as a practical textile printer this book could not have been written.

Coventry, 1969   Stuart Robinson

ORIGINS

The development of block printing on cloth until 1750

Many historians have surmised that printed textiles were made in the Caucasus around 2000 BC. Certainly by 450 BC the Greek historian Herodotus describes animal figures painted in pigment colours on the clothes of the tribes of that region. Printing blocks are said to have been used in India as far back as 3000 BC, although no such blocks or textiles have survived. We can only estimate from wall carvings, paintings or accounts, none of which can be assumed to be accurate. We have evidence of printing in India during the fourth century BC and the export of such fabrics to China, where they were much used and admired and, later, imitated.

Some scholars hold the opinion that India was the original home of the earliest printed textiles and certainly many examples found in other parts of the world came from India as part of the great export trade that country carried on from earliest times. This spread by land and sea to the Black Sea and Mediterranean peoples, by way of the Persian Gulf and the Red Sea to the Levant, and continued along the Nile to cover Egypt and North Africa and the Greek and Roman ports. The Greek geographer Strabo (63 BC–AD 20) records Indian printed textiles. It is not certain if Pliny the Elder (AD 23–79) in his *Natural History*, after discussing wax painting on cloth, then refers in a later passage to the printing of patterns on cloth. He mentions that 'after fulling, the white materials are painted, not with colours, but with substances that absorb the pigments'. These, he states, vary so that when the treated cloth is placed in a vat containing only one dye it comes out in many durable and differing colours.

The fabrics most commonly used were cotton, linen and silk; they were singed, close cropped, bleached or dyed a plain background colour before printing. Where the colour was applied directly from a block this was done by inking the block from a pad and pressing it on to the cloth by hand or by striking the back with a wooden mallet. It should be remembered that the traditional methods of textile printing in the Orient involved printing either a resist or a mordant upon the prepared cloth. If a starch or wax resist was used, the printed portions kept white when the fabric was later dipped in a dye vat. If, however, a mordant was printed, only the mordanted parts took the dye when immersed in the dye vat, later rinsing removing the surplus dye from the background areas. Both methods gave complete penetration of the fabric where so desired.

The early European textile printer failed to obtain such colouring of the fabric, merely impressing what was usually just a pigment dyestuff on to one side of the cloth.

It was only in the last decade of the nineteenth century that Robert Forrer first published his monumental researches into the origins of textile printing. Previously it had been assumed that little cloth printing existed before the sixteenth century. Forrer's work established that printed fabrics of excellent design and technique were known at the beginnings of the Christian era. Forrer excavated many sites along the banks of the Nile and particularly in the burial field of Achmim, the ancient city of Panopolis in Upper Egypt. Here was found the earliest printed textile known, dating from the fourth century AD. This was not the usual fragment remaining in such graves, but a complete child's tunic of white linen printed in blue with a diamond-shaped block containing a star-shaped design, arranged so as to leave a white grid all-over pattern (see plate 1).

The making up of this garment shows that it came from a length of printed fabric. An actual printing block of the same period was also discovered, consisting of a small cylindrical piece of wood about 2 in. long and 1½ in. in diameter, with simple patterns carved on each end. Another block of the seventh or eighth century made from sycamore wood, and showing stylized peacocks and the Tree of Life, was evidently used in repeat patterns. It is of special interest in that it was found in a tomb. It is well known that, from earliest times, it was customary to place in the tombs articles to indicate the profession and rank of the dead. It seems reasonable to suppose that this tomb was one of a textile printer, and that textile printing was an accepted craft at this period. The earliest two-colour print was also found at Achmim and dates from the sixth century AD. This print is indicative of an exceedingly advanced stage of technical ability, four different wooden blocks being required to obtain the three-colour effect on the unbleached cotton (see plates 2–4).

Other printed textiles, printed in red, black and powdered gold, have been found in Persia (sixth and seventh centuries); others have been found in Ancon in Peru and in ancient Mexico. This form is still practised by South American Indians along the Orinoco river, where earthen stamps are used by the women to print patterns on their breasts and hips.

The Polynesian islands continue a very primitive form of fabric decoration known as tapa printing in which patterns are printed in oil-soot pigments upon a non-woven bark or bast cloth. This fabric, closely allied in the methods of manufacture to paper-making, is the bark-fibre cloth of Central Africa and the South Seas. It is formed by the prolonged soaking of the bark of certain trees including the paper mulberry, the bread fruit, the fig tree and the hibiscus bush in water, which is then beaten to the required width and thickness with wooden beaters carved with intricate patterns. It is often decorated with painted or printed patterns in many colours and made into ordinary clothing or ceremonial hangings.

The fabric was also widely used in North West America, in ancient Central

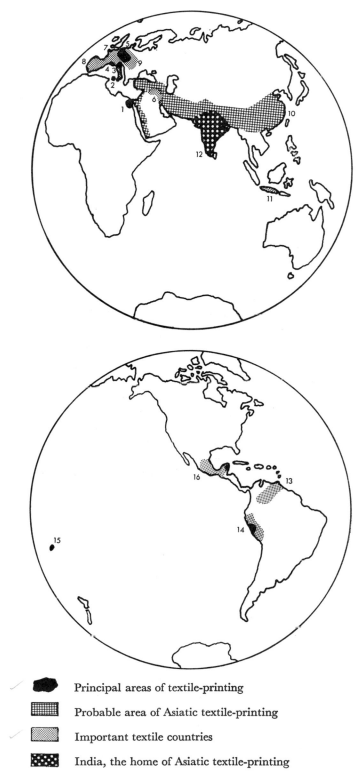

1 Egypt (Achmim)
2 Sicily (Palermo)
3 Italy (Venice)
4 Arles
5 Germany (Cologne,
  Düsseldorf, Mainz,
  Strassburg, Augsburg,
  Nuremberg)
6 Sassanid Persia
7 France
8 Spain
9 Austria
10 China
11 Java
12 India
13 Orinoco district
14 Peru (Ancon)
15 Samoa Islands
16 Mexico

1a. Textile printing up to the year 1500. Compiled by Gustav Schaefer and courtesy *CIBA Review.*

■ Principal areas of textile-printing

▦ Probable area of Asiatic textile-printing

▒ Important textile countries

▨ India, the home of Asiatic textile-printing

9

America down to the Andes and Amazon and the Grand Chaco region, where, in the main, it existed along with traditional weaving techniques. It is also found in Malaya, Java and other parts of the East Indies.

Its most extensive use was in the vast region known as Oceania. Apart from Australia, where except for a few northern districts using bark as distinct from bast cloth, the aborigines were too primitive for even such elementary techniques, this method for the manufacture of cloth was used in the innumerable islands scattered over an area several times larger than Europe. It contained some of primitive man's highest civilizations, all of which were totally destroyed as distinctive cultures by the coming of the white man.

The relatively simple techniques are now only practised on a commercial tourist trade basis.

After manufacture, the papery cloth was often dyed and then printed with blocks which were either constructed from leaves or made from a hard wood engraved with fine patterns. Other forms were painted with designs using bamboo pens, grass or twig brushes dipped in dye. A more complicated type used a matrix or curved board, bearing either engraved patterns or patterns embossed from pandanus leaves, which was placed under the stretched fabric and dye rubbed into the grooves. Local earths gave white, red and black. It is more unusual to find blues and greens.

In Europe, the first known example also dates from the sixth century and was found in the tomb of Saint Caesarius of Arles (502–43) in France. It may be Egyptian in origin. A similar piece was found in 1104 in the tomb of St Cuthbert at Durham. In the Magna Charta, the great charter of English personal and political liberty obtained from King John in 1215, the thirty-fifth chapter mentions the cloth and dyeing trades when it renews a decree passed in 1197 by King Richard I called the Assize of Cloth. This established uniform standards of dyeing and confined trading in dyed cloths to the larger towns and rural parishes. Most of the lower classes were thus left with the use of the common grey cloths.

Although Clouzot in *Painted and Printed Fabrics* mentions block printing in Italy in the thirteenth century, there seems to be a long interval in which it is not possible to trace any continuous development between the resist methods such as wax batik and indigo starch printing from blocks and the use of a block to print the actual dye. Neither can it be taken for granted that the later use of blocks for the printing of cloth with pigments or inks was a mere modification of the printing on paper for books. Yet craft techniques do not always develop in a logical manner. Other considerations prevent this and it is likely that the dyes available to the early medieval printers were unsuited to application from a block. Resist printing with a wax or starch paste was highly suitable, but only the insoluble pigments (indigo ground with lead and water, gold and silver metallic powders, ruddle or red ochre, and black pine soot ground in oil and mixed with varnish) could be used to give reasonably fast printing for hangings.

According to an Italian record, the wood used for the blocks was walnut or pear and the work was often carried out in monasteries. It is revealing to note that no cloth printers' guild was known in the Middle Ages. Such craftsmen had to join one of the guilds for the painters, the joiners or the goldsmiths. The actual names of cloth printers, in fact, do not appear until records of around 1500, and then it is often noted that the printer printed books as well as cloth (see diagrams 1a and b).

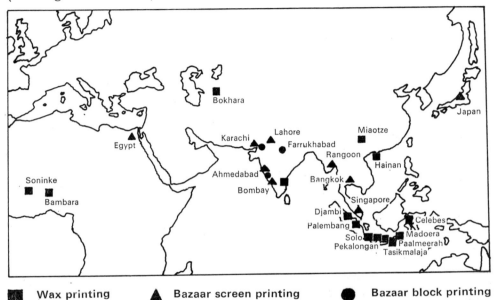

	Wax printing	▲	Bazaar screen printing	●	Bazaar block printing

1b. Main centres of craft printing of textiles. Courtesy I.C.I. (Dyestuffs Division).

In the early Middle Ages the blocks were small and usually printed in one colour only, on undyed fabric, but by the tenth century the fabric was often dyed and then printed in one or more colours, including gold and silver. The craft seems to have arisen primarily out of the desire to produce cheap imitations of the rare and expensive textiles that came over the caravan or sea routes from the Near and Far East. A document issued in Nuremberg about 1450 gives clear instructions on the copying of flowers and animals from cloth of gold. The cloth of gold fabrics were magnificent brocades from the Orient and Italy. Prints copying these rich designs provided cheap substitutes for the lesser monasteries, churches and middle-class houses. Owing to their poor fastness to washing, these were hardly suitable for clothing.

To economize further the number of small blocks was kept to the minimum by inserting touches of colour with a brush, or painting in solid areas of colour within printed outlines. Gold and silver dust was often scattered over the printed pigments before they had time to dry. Velvet effects were obtained by spreading powdered wool on the gummed ink pattern while it was still wet, and powdered selinite was sometimes applied to the whole of a hanging to enrich the lustre.

In the twelfth century districts of the lower Rhine specialized in producing cloths with strong Byzantine and Near Eastern influences upon the closely knit all-over designs. Similar influences are apparent in later Portuguese fabrics with bird and human figure patterns.

As well as printing with small blocks, the fourteenth century saw the development of large blocks that combined a number of separate pattern forms. A block 8 in. × 24 in. and dating from the end of the fourteenth century, was found at Sennecy in France; it was too large for the known paper size of the time, but this would appear to be exceptional (see plate 16).

These blocks often imitated the design of woven fabrics, and as embroidery became much more popular, blocks were used to print cloth with outline patterns. This practice coincided with an interest in figure designs of a formal or heraldic nature within a frame, and an extension to six, eight, ten or more large blocks in a variety of colours for such articles as altar cloths, wall hangings, coverings for relics, floor cloths, lining of church vestments and the like. An important centre for this type of printing in the late Middle Ages was Venice. The earliest known pictorial print from Venice is the so-called tapestry of Sion, dating from the late fourteenth century. It is a mural hanging, printed in oil colours on linen. Red is used for the bands of line patterns containing medallions of busts or fabulous animals, and black for a number of pictures showing a procession of dancing men and women, another row of battle scenes and a third row depicting the story of Oedipus. The printer has made such mistakes as accidentally inverting a block or omitting parts of the border (see plate 10).

Many patterns used religious motifs possibly derived from the art forms stimulated by the Renaissance in Italy (see plate 9).

The practice of making transfer patterns from embroidery spread the craft from the ecclesiastical into the commercial world. There was still, however, little link between the cutting and use of wood blocks for resist printing, for picture production and for cloth printing. Each craftsman was kept away from the dyer by the exclusiveness of the guild system, which encouraged guilds jealously to guard their own secrets. It was not until a more settled economy and further exploration by Portuguese and Venetian merchant adventurers brought greater imports of foreign textiles, particularly from the East, that this stranglehold was relaxed and new methods and equipment were invented to satisfy the ever-growing demand for patterned cloth, but at a more reasonable cost than the imported textiles (see diagram 2).

The greatest obstacle to the improvement in output, apart from the guild system, was in the total manual nature of the craft. In the earliest methods, the block was pressed upon the fabric by hand alone and the prints so obtained show great variation in the take-up of the pigment upon the cloth. *A Book of the Arts or Treatise on Painting*, written in the late fourteenth century by Cennino Cennini, gives precise instructions for the making of blocks with handles, the application to the block of varnish-thickened dye by means of a glove, and the block printing done between two benches with the block resting on top of the

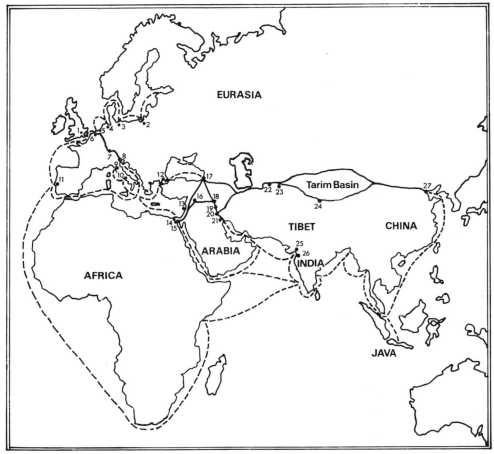

2. Important medieval trade routes by land and sea. Compiled by Gustav Schaefer, courtesy *CIBA Review.*

1 London 2 Danzig 3 Lubeck 4 Bremen 5 Amsterdam 6 Rotterdam 7 Basle 8 Venice 9 Pisa 10 Amalfi 11 Lisbon 12 Constantinople 13 Damascus 14 Alexandria 15 Cairo 16 Palmyra 17 Trebizond 18 Mosslu 19 Samarra 20 Baghdad 21 Busra 22 Bokhara 23 Samarkand 24 Yarkand 25 Cambay 26 Broach 27 Peking.

fabric and a small wooden block rubbed against the underneath of the fabric.

In later times the pressure was applied by hand rollers and iron hammers; the latter form is still in use in hand-block printing today. As blocks became larger registration and evenness of printing became more difficult and the gradual use of starch and thickening agents, aqueous solutions or suspensions to carry other than pigment dyes, further complicated the task of the printer of cloth.

Other factors, however, also influenced the development of textile printing, and since these were both political and economic they were outside the control of the printer himself. The fibre used was often cotton or coarse linen, which were first adopted as a cheap substitute for the costly woven silk brocades, damasks and velvets. The patterns used on these so-called 'false tapestries' attempted to imitate the richness and opulence suggested by more exotic materials. The rise in the standard of living in the early sixteenth century, however, decreased the popularity of cotton goods, since many more people could afford silk or wool.

The first authentic document in which cotton is mentioned appears as a petition of 1620, now in the London and Guildhall Library: 'about twenty years past diverse people in this Kingdome, but chiefly in the countie of Lancashire, have found out the trade of making of other Fustians, made of a kind of Bombast or Downe, being a fruit of the earth growing upon little shrubs or bushes, brought into this Kingdome by the Turkey merchants, from Smyrna, Cyprus, Aora, and Sydon, but commonly called cotton wool . . . and also of Lynnen Yarne most part brought out of Scotland . . . There is at the least 40 thousand pieces of Fustian of this kind yearly made in England . . . and thousands of poor people set on working of these Fustians.'

A petition by a Maurice Peeters of 1610 denounces daily fraudulent practices 'in the manufacture of bombazine cotton, such as groweth in the land of Persia, being no kind of wool' (State Papers, Dom., LIX. 5).

By 1640 the cotton industry was well established in the Manchester area, importing 'cotton wooll' through London from Cyprus and Smyrna, to spin, weave and dye into fustians, vermilions and dymities which were sold in London. Manchester had been well known for its bleaching, fulling, dyeing and finishing from as early as 1295, when a dyer, Alexandre le Tinctore de Mamecestre, is mentioned in a contract of sale of land. In 1540 the rural weavers of Lancashire produced coarse woollen stuffs of a frieze type known as Manchester cottons (in this sense, cotton is used to mean down or nap, and is unconnected with the name for the fibre which is derived from the Arabic *qutun*). Wool and linen were regularly processed at this time.

The development of a suitable environment for the later establishment of printing in the Lancashire area that came about in the 1750s was helped by this long association with the allied processes. The medieval textile trade enjoyed the King's protection, and the relative weakness of the guild system in Manchester permitted an influx of skilled immigrants in the late 1580s, after the siege and capture of Antwerp by Alexander Farnese. Apart from silk, which was a traditionally aristocratic fibre requiring a resident court patronage lacking in this area, the absence of guild restraint encouraged the immigrants in a great variety of styles including many mixed fabrics. Defoe in his *Tour through the Whole Island of Great Britain* (1724–7) mentions the long trains of heavily loaded pack animals transporting cotton and other goods from Manchester to numerous fairs and markets. A popular fabric was fustian (linen warp/cotton weft, first mentioned in England in 1554 as *fustian de Naples* and also produced in a finer quality with a worsted yarn), exempted from the 1721 prohibition by an act of 1735 on the ground that it was 'a branch of the ancient fustian manufacture'.

The eventual change in public taste dated from 1592, when an English privateer brought into Devonport a Spanish ship with its cargo of calicoes, lawns, quilts, carpets and other luxury goods. The flamboyant colouring, fast dyes and skilled design of the printed and painted cloths decided English merchants to form the London East India Company. Their charter was granted in 1600, and they soon established direct communications with the Indies over, amongst other goods, the so-called calicoes (a corruption of Calicut, the Indian port of origin). A Dutch company followed in 1602 and Colbert established a French company in 1664.

It was not until the early seventeenth century that the importing into Europe by the various companies of quantities of fast-dyed, multi-coloured Indian and Dutch East Indian printed and painted cottons or chintz brought about a revival in the popularity of cotton. As soon as the fashionable ladies saw these *toile peinte* or *indiennes, chites* (from Chitagong in Bengal), *suratas* (Surat, north of Bombay) and *patnas* (Patna on the Ganges), as they became known to them, they insisted on decorated gowns. The gentlemen wore dressing-gowns of these painted cloths and this fashion became even more widespread after the visit of the Siamese envoys to the court of Louis XIV at Versailles in 1684. The *indiennes*, the *siamaises* and the *perses* were in vogue, but very expensive. Yet the fashion was so overwhelming that the demand could not be satisfied by normal trade and many attempts were made in various parts of Europe to produce imitations of these Indian prints and calicoes.

At first the attempts to provide cheap substitutes were in no way equal to the brilliantly dyed and patterned fabrics of the East. The workmen lacked both the skill in painting and the technical knowledge of dye fastness, so that the crude imitations of the Oriental fabrics, although using wax-resist and woodblock printing for the outlines, together with hand filling-in of other colours, bore no comparison at all with their subtle originals. It was not until the 1670s that a successful industry was established. This used wooden blocks, at times with metal inserts, but combined these with the Indian methods of mordant dyeing.

In England, William Sherwin, an engraver of West Ham, took out a patent in 1676, 'A grant for fourteen years of the invention of a new and speedy way for producing broad calico, which being the only true way of the East India printing and stayning such kind of goods', and by 1700 the industry was flourishing in south-eastern England near to good water supplies, particularly at Richmond, Poplar, West Ham, Lambeth, Bermondsey, Wapping, Bromley by Bow on the river Lea and later at Old Ford. The revocation of the Edict of Nantes in 1685 drove many French Huguenots to this country, and amongst the silk weavers, felt-hat makers, goldsmiths and silversmiths were a number of textile printers. One of these, a Frenchman from Holland, established the first English calico-printing factory at Richmond, then known as West Sheen, around 1690. This was a flourishing business and employed many workers, both men and women. Other establishments of note included that at Bromley by Bow, which led to the famous Bromley Hall, which was first mentioned in the 1740s, and that of Robert Jones at Old Ford.

The first reaction to the immense popularity of these cotton prints came from the already established wool and silk merchants. Not unnaturally, they felt great alarm at the invasion of their territory by such an overwhelming swing to cotton. So, quite unexpectedly, the French Government imposed a very strict decree on 24 October 1686 which forbade the wearing of the *toiles de coton peintes dux Indes ou contrefailes dans Le Royaume.*

Similar conditions to those in France prevailed in England, where in 1701 the silk and wool weavers obtained a ban upon imported Indian printed calicoes, followed in 1720 by a prohibition upon the use in this country of all cotton printed in England. From then until 1774 the printers were restricted to printing for export or using mixture fabrics such as a cotton weft and linen warp for printing for the home market. In this period riots of weavers, and fines on women for wearing chintz gowns were frequent. Yet despite this opposition, the industry still survived with silk-cotton or linen-cotton fabrics as well as the permitted printing in one colour only.

The exception of fustians from the Act gave the Manchester craftsmen an opportunity to develop a finer form of mixed fibre much to the 'grievous distress' of the Norwich woollen manufacturers, who lost an action they brought against the Manchester weavers in 1735 claiming that the printed fustians being sold infringed the Act.

Sir Richard Arkwright's invention of an improved spinning frame resulted in a new trade in all-cotton English calico produced from his first spinning mill worked by water power, established in 1771. This in turn caused the repeal of the restrictions in 1774, although leaving heavy excise duties until 1831.

Foreigners who settled in parts of London often established small one-man calico dyeing and printing businesses. A most attractive trade card of the late seventeenth century advertises the business of John Wildblood which he carried on at the sign of The Rainbow and Three Pigeons in St Clement's Lane off Lombard Street. Of interest is the unusual statement that he had married the widow of another silk dyer named Harrington. Another trade card shows printer Jacob Stampe at work. Although he obviously printed anything within his ability, he was principally a 'fashion' printer of calicoes. This meant that he did not provide the fabric he printed; this was brought by his customers and he then printed stock designs, probably in black pigment outline with other colours added by hand. Many of the craftsmen were journeymen who travelled around from inn to inn, working in outhouses and disused stables until they had satisfied local demand, when they and their boy apprentices and family moved on. They operated in much the same way as the goldsmiths and silversmiths of that time, who would take the metal brought to them and charge for the 'fashioning' of it. Fashion textiles came into being in this manner (see plates 14 and 39).

Another interesting card of this period was possibly engraved by the noted engraver George Bickham (died *c.* 1758); it is now in the collection of Sir

Ambrose Heal. It stated that 'C. Hooker, Callico Printer, At the Anchor and Crown in Ratcliff-high-Way, between Old and New Gravel Lane, PRINTS all Sorts of Linnen in all Colours (the printing of which is allow'd by Act of Parliament) from Three Pence (the Duty excepted) to Twelve Pence which will hold washing. HE ALSO scours stiffens and glazes all sorts of Callicos, for Beds, Window-Curtains, Room-Hangings, Gowns, etc at reasonable Rates'.

His versatility is shown by the remainder of the card: 'N.B. An Eminent Physician in the Cure of AGUES, after many Years Practice and Success on Thousands, being unwilling a Remedy so valuable Should be lost at his Decease, which he had never known to fail did therefore communicate ye SECRET to ye above mention'd who for 16 Years past has in a private Manner apply'd it to several hundreds with like Success; And having been often solicited to advertise the Publick, of a Remedy so very useful in that dolorous DISTEMPER, he takes this opportunity to assure them who labour under it, that they may have a perfect Cure upon taking of this Electuary with out the return of another Fit, tho' it has been of ever so long standing; and which is so inoffensive, it may be safely given to Women with Child, as has been often practis'd.

'PERSONS IN MEAN CIRCUMSTANCES WILL BE CUR'D FOR 5 SHILS.'

The shops that sold printed and dyed goods also issued business cards, and Mary and Ann Hogarth had their card designed by the famous William Hogarth around the middle of the eighteenth century. By the early nineteenth century trade cards, such as those of Joseph Carter, show the general nature of family businesses that had now developed, as well as the relatively new numbering of streets brought in at this time (see plate 10).

GREAT BRITAIN: 1750 TO THE PRESENT DAY

Copper-plate and wood-block prints

The status of the English cloth printer changed dramatically in the mid-eighteenth century with the development of printing from engraved metal plates which enabled the printer to use considerably larger repeat units with greater detail of fine engraving than could be obtained with wood blocks.

Early designs of the simplest type, such as a geometrical form, a leaf or an arabesque shape, were roughly printed in crude pigment colours from engraved relief plates. Stamped by hand on linen, calico or fustian, these were, according to O'Brien's *The British Manufacturers Companion and Calico Printers' Assistant* published in 1792, sold at 3s to 3s 6d a yard. A square yard would require a 10 in. × 5 in. block to be applied about fifty-two times.

The method was brought by Francis Nixon from Drumcondra, near Dublin, to Merton, Surrey, England, where he established a works in 1756. At first not only were metal plates used but additional colours were often added with smaller wood blocks or painted in by a technique called 'pencilling'. The technique was so admired that a number of other printers developed its use and many of their designs and names are known to us. Among the most famous are Robert Jones (at Old Ford, Poplar, around 1760–80), John Collins (formerly of Temple-Oge, near Dublin, but settled in Woolmers, Hertfordshire, by 1765/6), Talwin and Foster (the Bromley Hall printworks on the river Lea, 1694–1823) and many others in and around London, particularly John Munns (calico-printer and gunpowder-maker, 1760s to 1784), the Wares and Vint & Gilling of Crayford, Kent, and in Lambeth and Wallington.

In other parts of the country the methods were established at Aberdeen (1720s), Edinburgh (1729), Glasgow (1738), Bolton (1751), Bamber Bridge (1760), Carlisle (1761), Preston and Oswaldtwistle (1764).

This increasing expansion in other areas at the expense of the London printers was helped by two other factors which eventually led to the closure of most of the London works. One factor was the invention of the first successful rotary printing machine patented by the Scotsman Thomas Bell in 1783. The second was the proximity of the Lancashire printers to the weavers of the new English all-cotton cloth who had benefited from Arkwright's patents of the 1770s and Cartwright's invention of the power loom. By 1820 only handkerchief and a few other forms of specialized printing remained in London. The bulk of textile printing had moved to Lancashire and Carlisle, where it has remained to this day. Only a few firms such as Arthur Sanderson and Co. have established print works near to London in this century.

Pattern books of the period, now in the Musée de L'Impression sur Étoffes at Mulhouse and also in the Victoria and Albert Museum in London, show that many Dublin and London printers were producing outstanding copper-plate prints well before Christophe Philippe Oberkampf in France (in the late 1770s). The designs included commemorative prints, pastoral, military, political and theatrical scenes as well as large flower, bird and figure designs. Towards the end of the century pictorial prints based on engravings of country scenes by such artists as George Morland (1763–1804) were very much in favour. The colours were derived in the main from madder for black, red, purple and brown and extended after 1740 with indigo blue and weld yellow and their mixtures. Later on further common dyestuffs came into use which gave reds from Brazilwoods (not a very fast colour, derived from various leguminous trees, including lima, sapan and peach wood, often used to heighten the red of madder); brilliant, if impermanent yellows from turmeric, a powder obtained from the ground-up tubers of *Curcuma tinctoria*, a plant found in India and other Eastern countries. As Berthollet remarked, 'The shade arising from the Turmeric is not long of disappearing in the air'. Blue came from woad (*Isatis tinctoria*), which, although not as brilliant as indigo, is even more permanent. It was widely distributed as a crop in Europe, Asia and North Africa and was the only blue dye in the West before indigo was introduced from India. The process of preparation as a cloth dye was complicated, employing only the leaves. It was cultivated in Lincolnshire until World War I. Violet was produced from orchil or archil (*Rocella tinctoria*), a substantive or non-mordant dye obtained from lichens growing on rocks in the Canary Islands and other tropical and subtropical areas of the Levant. The dye, produced by the action of ammonia and oxygen (present in putrid urine and slaked lime) upon the crushed lichens was not very fast, despite the tempting rich shades produced. It was first brought to Europe in the early fourteenth century. Cochineal (*Coccus cacti*, the dried bodies of an insect, some 70,000 to 1 lb, giving a wide variety of red shades) gave scarlet. It came to Europe from the Americas, but recent discoveries in the Ararat valley and adjacent areas suggest it was known and used by the Assyrians before the seventh century BC (see plates 32 and 33).

The printers used these dyes with a variety of mordants and chemicals on a trial-and-error basis, without any full knowledge of the chemistry employed, or what actually took place during the printing. The fabric was usually bleached in the open air to give a white background, and thus the maximum brilliance, to the printed colours. The printing process involved a number of distinct methods, all of which might be used, or only a selection, to produce the finished cloth. These may be summarized as (1) to print directly on the cloth; (2) to dye the cloth an even background colour and remove this by printing a bleaching agent from the block on to the dyed background; (3) to print a mordant, or a variety of mordants, on the cloth in varying strengths, so that a dip in a dyebath will produce a wide variety of tones and shades within a group of colours (for example, black from an iron mordant, yellow, orange, red, purple, brown from their respective mordants); (4) to print a resist substance, often a starch paste or a wax, upon the cloth, to resist a dye applied from a dyebath or painted on (see plate 12).

The mordant and resist methods developed from the Indian styles and eventually superseded most of the other methods until the discovery of synthetic dyestuffs.

It was customary prior to 1810 to overprint yellow (from one of the dyewoods) on top of indigo to produce a green. From about 1820 a mineral blue with yellow overprinted was used. After about 1835 a mixed yellow and blue solid green dye was employed.

The final process involved the finishing of the fabric by imparting a glazed surface, sometimes called 'sleeking'. A curved flint block as large as a fist with a highly polished face was passed over the printed cloth, which lay in a trough shaped to fit the block. The cloth had been prepared by a bath in a thin solution of beeswax, both to help the final gloss and to diminish the danger of 'scrumping' (the permanent formation of small rucks in the cloth as it was polished). Glass and agate were also used for the sleeking stone (see plate 13).

This laborious process survived in a limited form until the early years of this century, when it gave way to roller polishing. Other methods are known such as 'paper bowl' glazing, 'rotary starch' machines and 'hot bed' methods.

After this period the standard of copper-plate printing rapidly deteriorated and the technique was used principally for the cheap commemorative prints so popular at this time. These ranged over many subjects: the death of Admiral Nelson at the Battle of Trafalgar in 1805; satirical comments on the 'brave' Corsican, the Emperor Napoleon, during the blockade of 1806–13; the Jubilee of George III in 1809; the Manchester Reform Meeting of 1819; the opening of the first railway line between Liverpool and Manchester in 1831; Lord John Russell's Reform Bill of 1832 and a most prosaic map of England in that year; the census of 1881; a variety of guild souvenir handkerchiefs and many other designs, including puzzles, lampoons, snuff cloths and 'lunch' wrappers. In general, however, the designs were crude and ill printed when compared with the products of the half-century previous to 1800 (see plates 20–22).

Of wood-block printing, which preceded copper plate and continued with it, few early examples have survived. Only designs remain of the many blocks executed by the leading designer of the time, Daniel Goddard. Wood blocks were adapted to rollers by Ebinger in France in 1800 and are usually known as Surface or Peg printing (see diagram 3). Later improved by Burch and also Cad and Hill, it was a distinct improvement on the Perrotine (q.v.); it could be adapted to print rainbow or fondu multi-colour printing (see diagram 4). A series of designs produced about 1750 by John Baptist Jackson (1701–77) show a continuously linked floral form. In other designs it is possible to trace an Indian

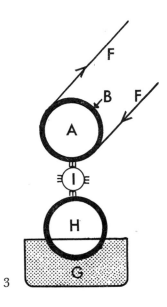

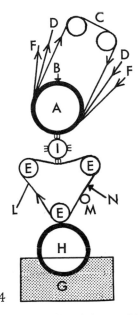

3   4

3. Ebinger's 'Surface' or 'Peg' block printing machine, 1800. The large roller A has a thick cotton lapping B around it to give resilience. The fabric to be printed F is carried round the roller A. The design is carved on a round roller I in relief (this gives it the appearance of pegs fixed to a round roller). The 'furnishing' roller H picks up the colour paste from the colour box G and transfers it to the design roller I which in turn prints it on to the fabric F.

4. Burch's improved form of Ebinger. The improvements add an endless thick backing blanket C, a 'back grey' cotton fabric D under the fabric F. In addition a 'furnishing' blanket N runs continuously around rollers in place of the Ebinger roller H; an adjustable tension roller M keeps the 'furnishing' blanket taut and a doctor blade L distributes the colour paste uniformly on the surface of the blanket H.

Cad and Hill's improved form was similar to Burch's but printed up to six colours simultaneously from six colour boxes, furnishing rollers and design rollers arranged in order around the larger roller A.

influence. As the Lancashire printers increased in number and importance they tended to concentrate upon polychrome wood-block prints. The subject-matter for these was infinite and the various refinements in dyes and dyeing processes were of particular importance.

One of the most important of these new discoveries was a direct method of printing with indigo rather than the several operations involving a wax-resist print, an indigo dyebath and a final de-waxing treatment. Much of our knowledge of the recipes of these times is to be found in such treatises as Edward Bancroft's (1744–1821) *Experimental Researches concerning the Philosophy of Permanent Colours* published in 1794 and in a revised edition in 1813. He also popularized the use of quercitron (the bark of a North American oak) as a fast yellow, which combined with indigo to give a range of very fast greens and, with madders, of good oranges.

Thomas Henry (1734–1816), an eminent chemist and experimental dyer of the period, reported in 1790 that 'the colours employed in the dyeing of fustians and cotten velvets were few; and even at this day, many of them are fugitive'.[1] As Dr Charlotte Luetkens suggests, these early limitations in England to pale shades on calico may have saved the industry from slavishly copying the rich elaborate Eastern designs before the techniques of roller printing were mastered.[2]

James Thompson of Clitheroe (1779–1850) was among the first to perfect a printed indigo discharge as well as a Turkey red discharge process. Walter Crum (1796–1867) is believed to have introduced resist printing. John Mercer of Oakenshaw (1791–1866) was prolific in his many inventions and solutions of difficult problems in dye chemistry. He is principally remembered as the inventor in 1850 of the process of mercerization. This treatment is based on the discovery that cotton fibres steeped for a short while in a strong solution of caustic soda swell and shrink in length. In this way the cellulose of which they are made acquires permanently a more dispersed or porous state. This gives the cotton fibres a greatly increased affinity for most dyes. (A later discovery by Horace Lowe in 1890, involving the holding of the fibres in a stretched state during the mercerization treatment, showed that they could also acquire a much higher and more permanent lustre.)

C. L. Berthollet (1748–1822), the eminent French chemist, in his *Essay on the new method of bleaching by means of oxygenated muriatic acid* . . . (translated by Robert Kerr and published in London in 1790), demonstrated the bleaching properties of chlorine. This was taken up by James Watt in this country and within a few years the sight of many acres of pieces of stuff spread out to bleach in the open air for months on end around all weaving villages vanished for ever.

Charles Taylor of Manchester, after a great deal of research, rediscovered around 1785 the secret of the dyes of the Near East and developed the famous Turkey reds, one of the most popular colours used by printers and dyers until the end of the nineteenth century.

In the late 1790s a calico printer of Indian muslins earned as much as 25s a week, whereas an agricultural labourer earned an average of 8s, cotton workers an average of 16s, and metalworkers 15s to 20s. Such high wages attracted rural workers to the printworks and other factories, which in turn caused an overcrowding of the labour market and a sharp drop in wages and conditions of employment. The availability of cheap labour reduced the number of apprentices, as can be seen in the *Journals of the House of Commons* for 1775–7, where it is stated that 'The trade does not require that all the men they employ should be brought up to it; common labourers are sufficient'. The introduction of machinery during the nineteenth century reinforced this attitude in a harsh manner and increased the split between the designer and the workman. The name 'apprentice' was often a pseudonym for cheap non-adult labour at as little as

[1] Henry, Thomas *Memorandum to Manchester Literary and Philosophical Society* 1790
[2] Luetkens, Dr C. *Ciba Review* 1962/2, pp 31 ff. An excellent series of articles on Manchester and the origins of Cottonopolis

3s 6d to 7s a week for as much work as the 25s of a workman. A petition in 1803 to reintroduce the apprenticeship system in calico printing was rejected by the House of Commons in 1807, despite much evidence submitted concerning the deterioration in the standards of craftsmanship and design.

From about 1810 onwards English and European chemists added to the previous dyestuffs that were based on the vegetable dyes madder, indigo and quercitron, not only new chemical resists and discharges, new recipes for the use of such colours as Prussian blue, cochineal and catechu and similar process innovations, but also an entirely new range of mineral colours which completely changed the colour palette in use at the beginning of the nineteenth century. In 1834 Friedlieb Ferdinand Runge (1795–1867) produced a new kind of dye from coal tar called kyanol.

Thus it can be seen that the use of natural dyestuffs for so many years did not change suddenly with the discovery of the coal-tar or aniline dye, mauveine, by Perkin in 1856. A gradual process of experimentation and discovery had taken place since the abandonment of the old pigment methods. This was to continue side by side with the increasing flood of new basic dyes such as magenta, alizarin and many others for some years to come. It was only the continual discovery of so many improved, faster and more brilliant synthetic dyes characterized by their greater purity and reliability that eventually rendered the subtle glowing colours of the natural dyes obsolete in commercial practice.

The elaborate flower, bird and curling foliage blocks of the late 1770s and 1780s changed at the peak of wood-block cutting in the 1790s to patterns on dark grounds or alternate light and dark stripes (see plate 27).

The next forty years is covered by a comprehensive collection of the designs and prints of the firm of Charles Swainson of Bannister Hall, near Preston, who were the leading printers of furnishings at this time. The series is now in the possession of Stead, McAlpin Ltd, of Carlisle, whose own records go back to 1750. The history of this firm has been traced by Bunt and Rose in *Two Centuries of English Chintz 1750–1950* and provides a fascinating picture of the development of one firm over a period of two hundred years (see plate 34).

The Swainson collection is particularly useful in showing the changes in wood-block printing from the fashionable dark madder grounds and careful drawing of the 1790s to the 'drab' style and freer treatment of 1800. White discharges on dark grounds with elaborate patterns of tiny dots were also popular at this time and were a direct result of the experiments going on to improve discharge printing (see plate 36).

In 1750 and 1757 William Chambers published engravings with Chinese pagodas and palace gardens. In 1726 a porcelain designer, J. G. Höroldt of Meissen, published Chinese engravings. Earlier, Jean Antoine Fraisse, the painter to the French Court, published a book of samples based on the collections of Oriental prints and fabrics in the possession of Prince Condé at Chantilly. The engraver and publisher Gabriel Huquier (1695–1772) had also issued albums *à la chinoise* full of exotic themes of birds, plants and figures. He had engraved for

Antoine Watteau (1687–1721), the famous painter who had used Chinese designs in his decorations for *La Muette* hunting lodge. Watteau commenced his career as a designer in a textile factory and can be said to be one of the originators of the great craze for Oriental and exotic designs that swept over Europe around the turn of the century. Such albums and engravings were an inexhaustible source of design for the decoration of textiles, porcelain and ceramics (see plate 29).

A quick succession of fashions followed from 1805, with the exotic designs based on classical, Indian, Egyptian, Chinese and similar sources giving way to bold and flamboyant designs of game birds, palm treees, Gothic and classical architectural features. Specialized forms during this period were a brightly coloured handkerchief style called 'lapis' employing a so-called 'resist-red' of 1810 and the printing in the early nineteenth century of centre panels for patchwork quilts. These were followed in the 1860s by numerous derivative designs with little feeling or pattern value. They were either cheap prints for the various overseas markets or copies of Continental fabrics specially brought over from France and intended for the middle and upper classes. Owen Jones's *Grammar of Ornament* (1856) provided a further source of 'historic ornament' for designs.

Two circumstances helped to contribute to the almost total degeneration in design after 1835. One was the introduction into the dyer's range of a most unpleasant solid green and a very ugly Russell brown in place of the old softer colours. The other was a growing tendency to overcrowd designs with a proliferation of irrelevant and random units often totally unrelated to the main pattern forms.

These factors, together with the worsening social and industrial conditions of calico printers at this time produced a most unhappy situation of *laissez-faire*. It was only in a few firms that the example of such millowners as David Dale in the 1780s, and his manager Robert Owen, was followed. Most calico printers catered for the increase in consumer demands for ever cheaper and cheaper cottons and only a few pursued the better-quality markets which demanded high standards of craftsmanship.

In 1719, when the agitation from the woollen manufacturers to have the prohibition on the wearing of Indian prints extended to the home-produced prints upon Indian cotton, there were some thirty calico printers in the London area. One of the largest of these, J. Mauvillion, employed around 200 workmen in his two printing establishments at Wandsworth and Mitcham, but the contemporary estimates give the figure of around 800–900 people working in calico printing at this time.

Potter gave the number of printworks in Great Britain in 1851, exclusive of the London district, as 202. In 1840 he estimated the comparable total as 166. He attributed the small increase to the difference between the average production of hand block printing of six pieces (168 yds) per day compared with the 200–500 pieces (5,600 to 14,000 yds) machine printed per day. Machines printed with infinitely fewer defects of printing and in many colours, up to ten or fifteen. He also gives interesting figures of the export drive of 1851, of the popularity of certain patterns produced by his firm and much other historical information.

Dr A. Schwarz in *CIBA Review* 1968/1 gives a very clear account of the pros and cons of the evolution of mills and factories.

'The working conditions in the early mills and print-shops of the late eighteenth and early nineteenth centuries were as bad and unhygienic as those already mentioned [those suffered by the slave-girl weavers of ancient Egypt]. Cleanliness was of no importance and no attempt was made to keep down the dust . . . Windows were kept closed at all times.' And, as a medical report upon a fever epidemic in 1784 among Lancashire mill-hands describes, although the mills and works were certainly very big buildings they had been planned to contain the maximum number of floors: 'The ceilings were as low as possible and the machines used considerable amounts of oil.' The air within these restricted and crowded spaces 'was full of dust from the fabrics which, settling on the oil, gave off a penetrating stench'.

This was in direct contrast to conditions in the U.S.A., where industrialization did not necessarily result in squalor at home or at work. Charles Dickens bore witness to this after his 1842 tour of the States.

Roller and rotary printing

One of the earliest attempts to design a continuous printing machine that is known to us is that described by Glorez of Moravia in 1701 which embodied a wooden printing roller to which the colour was applied from a pad. In 1743 Keen and Platt had invented a three-colour roller printing machine and Adkin secured a patent for a single-colour printing machine employing a roller in 1772. J.-A. Bonvallet, a textile printer of Amiens, used a machine for printing wool and plush in the 1770–80 period that consisted of an upper wooden roller and a lower hollow iron one with an engraved copper surface. Red-hot coals or iron balls were placed in the lower roller, which rotated in a colour trough and was pressed by an ingenious system of weights, levers and wheels against the upper roller which carried the cloth (see plate 15).

Many other attempts to use the mechanical principle of rotation in cloth printing were made at this period. One early device was used by Sir Robert Peel (1750–1830), next door neighbour of James Hargreaves (1720–78) and father of the nineteenth-century statesman, whose firm of Peel and Co was one of the leading calico printers of the 1790s to 1820s. He produced a famous pattern, Stormont Pins, by spraying dots of colour from a very large withy broom. To make the dots more regular in size and spacing, the broom was made into a cylindrical brush of the same width as the cloth, the tips of the bristles just dipping into the dye tray. As the brush revolved a ruler held across the bristles flicked the dots of colour on to the cloth. This was later replaced with a wooden roller carrying metal teeth.

In 1770 Charles Taylor and Thomas Walker invented a new method of printing cotton and linen by means of wooden rollers.

In 1783, the Scotsman Thomas Bell, working at Livesey, Hargreaves Hall and Company's Mosney works near Preston, patented a method of printing from engraved cylinders which was a decisive and revolutionary step forward. Although his machine has been subjected to numerous improvements, the principle was so basic that it has been retained (see diagram 5). By 1785 his six-colour machine was in production near Preston and was capable of doing the work of about forty hand printers and a further sixty auxiliary workmen. By the 1870s machines with as many as sixteen rollers were in use (see diagram 6). Bell

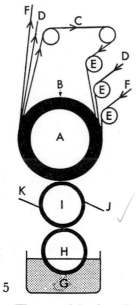

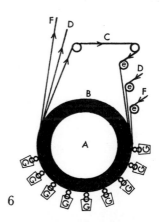

5. The essentials of a roller printing machine. The pressure cylinder A is covered with several layers of fabric B to make it resilient. An endless thick blanket C gives extra resilience which is protected from colour staining by the 'back grey' cotton fabric D, guided on by rollers E, as are C and F—the fabric being printed. The colour or dye-paste in the colour box or trough G is picked up by the 'furnishing' roller H which transfers it to the printing roller I carrying the design. (In some machines H transfers to a loose distributing blanket, running endlessly around small rollers, which then transfers to I.) Roller I continuously prints on fabric F which moves forward together with back grey D and blanket C. The doctor blade J scrapes excess colour off roller I, and another doctor K scrapes off lint and any loose impurities picked up by I from the fabric. (See plate 88.)

6. A multi-roller nine colour printing machine, basically the same as diagram 5 but able to print up to eighteen colours all carefully adjusted to register accurately one after the other.

was probably the first inventor to fit a steel blade or 'doctor' to remove the surface colour from the printed rollers and still leave the engraved areas sufficient colour within the engraving to transfer to a continuous length of fabric. Further refinements included Burton and Parkinson's union machine of 1805, which printed from engraved and surface rollers simultaneously, the Duplex printing-machine which prints both sides of the fabric at the same time and other variations. This and many other improvements helped to establish Lancashire as the leader in the printed-textile industry. Many famous firms both of printers and engravers were founded in the 1850s. Their history has been recorded in monographs such as *Edmund Potter of Dinting Vale* and *The History of the Calico Print Works of Messrs Hargreaves, at Accrington.*

Although at first the new machines were employed to produce cheap mono-chrome dress prints with small patterns, by 1810 sufficient technical knowledge and experience had been accumulated to print large-scale furnishing fabrics.

In Scotland, Glasgow became a textile centre particularly associated with Turkey red, the dye obtained from madder. Carlisle continued printing with wood blocks, as did London, where by 1840 there were only a few areas remaining around Crayford in Kent that still printed silk squares and similar articles.

The designs of the early roller prints from the better-quality printers show a high standard of engraving. Many of them were stipple engraved with further colours added from blocks or surface rollers. Floral patterns were popular around 1800 and were followed by striped Regency type patterns often intended to link with the imported French furniture so popular at this time, in 1823 by the rainbow-style which printed stripes in bright colours blending at the edges, and in 1825 by floral/fern/creeper-type patterns. An outstanding example of engraving was the 1830 Lancashire series taken from Audubon's *Birds of America.* Around 1840 special brilliantly coloured prints for the Portuguese market were produced called Portuguese documents. After this time, however, a deteriora-tion of design, similar to that shown in block printing, appears and standards were dropped to permit the mass printing of cheap textiles for the home market as well as overseas buyers. In the same way the introduction of the newer dyes already mentioned brought gaudy colours into the printers' palettes as more colour ranges were required for each new design (see plates 35, 41 and 45).

The discovery of mauveine

A most influential development was the discovery, already mentioned, of mauveine or Tyrian purple, one of the first of a long series of dyes manufactured from coal tar which themselves heralded other classes of dyestuffs and dyeing processes. It led also to the interdependence of the textile and dye-making industries. These new dyes all arose from the experiments during the Easter holidays of 1856 of a young assistant research worker of eighteen, William Henry Perkin. His object had been to synthesize quinine and during his experiments he noticed that the black tarry product he had isolated also contained a coloured precipitate. Despite the advice of his teacher, Professor Hofman, a noted chemist who later also developed new coal-tar dyes such as magenta and the napthalene colours, the young Perkin started by testing out the dyeing and light-fastness properties of mauveine on silk and established his own coal-tar plant at Greenford Green near Harrow to the north west of London. After much disappointment in the pioneer work of converting coal-tar products into dyes, which had not before been carried out on a large scale, he satisfactorily solved most of the problems and the coal-tar industry was soon firmly established throughout the world, and particularly in Germany and France.

The new dyes required different treatment for each of the main natural fibres then in use, including cotton, silk, wool and linen. Much of the experimenting was on a hit-and-miss method during the early days, but later a high degree of standardization was achieved of the many thousands of colouring matters isolated. From these were produced a larger number of reliable dyes for a wide variety of fibres and dyeing methods.

The first coal-tar or basic dyes had a natural affinity for the dyeing of wool and silk which they did not possess for cotton, linen or other cellulosic fibres unless a mordant such as tannic acid or metallic salts was used. In 1868 the alizarine colours were announced by Graehe and Liebermann. In 1884 Bottiger discovered the azo dye Congo red, the first direct cotton dye which could dye cotton without a mordant. This is now one of the largest classes of dyestuffs.

Other classes gradually followed, such as the acid dyes particularly suitable for their application to wool and natural silk in an acid dyebath; mordant dyes useful for all fibres; pre-metallized dyes which do in one stage an operation that mordant dyes do in two; sulphur dyes for use with cellulose fibres; vat dyes of exceptional fastness to light, washing, perspiration and bleaching and widely used throughout the industry. These have been further increased since the discovery of synthetic man-made fibres.

The major development in dyestuffs since 1945 has been the introduction of a new class of reactive dyes. These dyes are applied by simple techniques to cotton, viscose rayon, nylon, natural silk and wool. They secure their brilliance and good fastness to light and washing by achieving a chemical linkage of the dye with the fibre during the fixation process.

The aftermath of the Industrial Revolution: The Great Exhibition; William Morris and the influence of the Arts and Crafts movement

Another influence that must be considered had very far-reaching effects. It began as a reaction against the aesthetic credo that had been built up since 1800, and in order to appreciate the effect on textile printing it is necessary to consider at some length the whole social and aesthetic climate at this period half-way through the nineteenth century.

That the conditions in factories by 1824 were as bad as, or even worse than, those described earlier is clearly stated in the writings of William Cobbett: 'In the cotton-spinning work these creatures are kept, fourteen hours each day, locked up, summer and winter, in a heat of from EIGHTY TO EIGHTY FOUR DEGREES.' He goes on to say that at this temperature in the harvest fields many men and horses dropped dead; 'they have . . . no cool room to retreat to . . . the door of the place wherein they work, is *locked*, except *half an hour* at tea-time; the work people are not allowed to send for water to drink in the hot weather.' He then gives a long list of fines published in many factories including 'Any spinner found with his window open . . . 1s.' 'Any spinner found washing himself . . . 1s.' 'Any Spinner leaving his oil can out of its place . . . 6d.' 'Any Spinner heard whistling . . . 1s.' 'Any two Spinners, *found together* in the *necessary*, each man 1s.' '. . . the pay . . . has to be laid out at a SHOP. That shop is, generally, . . . the master's', who also owned the cottages or cellars in which the workmen must live.[1]

Allowing for Cobbett's dramatic enthusiasm for broad contrasts and his statement that he did not like to see the machines lest this should help him to understand them, there is little reason to doubt that such conditions did exist in many textile factories.

Dr Coleman, in his monumental history of Courtaulds,[2] gives a graphic description of the attitude of the early Victorians, who felt that the tasks of attending the machinery of throwing-mills was neither difficult nor arduous, and peculiarly well suited to the children of the poor. In 1813 George Courtauld was busy recruiting parish children from workhouses to be bound apprentices. 'I had my choice of upwards of fifty girls of different ages and accepted all but one that were within the age of ten and thirteen . . . I really expect and earnestly hope

[1] Cobbett, William *Political Works* VI, 430–42: 'To the Landowners on the Evils of Collecting Manufacturers into Great Masses', 17 November 1824
[2] Coleman D. C. *Courtaulds, An Economic and Social History* Vol. I, pp 42–4 ff (these two volumes give a very good account of the growth of a textile firm from 1819 to 1941)

that by continued care and attention my establishment of apprentices will prove a nursery of respectable young women fitted for any of the humble walks of life.' He proposed to supervise these child workers with persons who would maintain 'perfect silence except the singing of hymns which we find a useful relaxation and a help to industry, attention and orderly conduct'. Dr Coleman adds that 'this musically alleviated toil was to be accompanied by a system of marks for blame or praise, exhibited on slates'. Courtaulds were among the better employers of their time and did try to provide welfare, education and help to those employees who merited it. Even so, by 1871, Samuel Courtauld drew an average annual income of £46,000 from the firm as part of his total income approaching £70,000. At the same time, he paid his foreman dyer £62 10s per annum, and one of his power-loom operators an average of £15 annually.

Such wages applied also to the textile-printing industry, where the conditions were often far worse, the premises old-fashioned and ill adapted to new machinery, and the position and authority of the craftsmen had been gradually whittled down and spread between many hands.

The Industrial Revolution enabled manufacturers, particularly those printing textiles, to turn out many thousands of yards of cheap designs in the same time as, and often at less cost than, one length produced by hand. Since the greatest items of cost were the designing and the block or plate cutting, the cost was reduced by copying foreign or earlier designs and by employing the quickest and crudest cutting or engraving. Examples are known where a copied pattern had not been adapted to a new width, but part of the pattern was arbitrarily cut away and so had destroyed the repeat. In this way the cost of adjusting the pattern had been saved. Skilled craftsmanship was replaced by mechanical repetition and haphazard filling of a space with patterns that bore little relevance to the fabric or its use. This caused the skilled craftsman or designer to withdraw in disgust from the attempts to satisfy the voracious demands of an ill-educated public. Industrialism was linked in the craftsman's mind with utility, with ugliness and with profit. The present time seemed unendurable, and the artist withdrew into his aloof tower and dreamt his dreams—dreams of the day when the artist was a craftsman, proud to work with his hands, recognized by all as a leader and benefactor. As he looked around all he saw was overornamented, vulgar and crude, whether it was architecture or industrial art and crafts. When he looked back into the past it was the Middle Ages that seemed to honour the artist and craftsman. The first glimmerings of 'art for art's sake', part of the doctrine enunciated by Victor Cousin (1792–1867), the French philosopher, and popularized by Theophile Gautier (1811–72), began to appear. It was felt that the craftsman of this time was shackled by the machine; he had become its tool and was no longer able to control it.

This feeling was particularly noticeable in the writings and lecturings of John Ruskin (1819–1900), the writer and art critic, who had great influence on the leading thinkers and designers of his day. In his work is to be found the constant reiteration that art, in the wide sense of the term, had lost its way since the

Renaissance, and particularly that the social foundations of art and crafts had crumbled with the disintegration of the whole pattern of life since the Industrial Revolution. In 1849 Ruskin declaimed: 'We want no new style of architecture. The forms of architecture already known to us are good enough for us.'[1] In order therefore to reform art, one must promote socialism, the principle that individual freedom should be completely subordinated to the interests of the community. Sometimes the principles were founded on Christianity, sometimes upon humanity. Always it was thought of as a literary-artistic movement and those who supported it usually possessed a highly developed social conscience.

At this period two important happenings occurred. The first was the attempt in 1848 of seven young men, including the artists William Holman Hunt (1827–1910), John Everett Millais (1829–96), and Dante Gabriel Rossetti (1828–82), to return to the 'ideality' of the painters before Raphael by founding the Pre-Raphaelite Brotherhood, a largely fortuitous choice of name, it must be added. It was a necessary reaction against both the traditional methods of teaching in the official art academies of Europe and the implications of mechanization inherent in the Industrial Revolution. The movement was at first markedly literary and started a short-lived periodical called, appropriately enough, *The Germ*. The Pre-Raphaelites insisted on the importance of a serious subject, elaborate symbolism and original illustration together with what, at that period, were startling technical innovations. Once their aims were known they were savagely attacked by critics who said they were setting up as better than Raphael, that they were secret Romanists (implying a connection with the Oxford Movement) and, as was elaborated by Dickens in his attack on Millais's *The Carpenter's Shop* shown at the Royal Academy of 1850, that they were blasphemers.

When Ruskin came to their defence in 1851 their critics relapsed into background murmurings, and the group, now accepted, but without any established theoretical basis, dissolved and informally refounded itself as a kind of second Brotherhood at Oxford, where Rossetti and Hunt joined with Edward Burne-Jones (1833–98) and William Morris (1834–96), a young man of independent means. This group was led by the handsome, brilliant Rossetti, son of a revolutionary refugee, an outstanding conversationalist, a pre-Raphaelite poet and painter with flowing dark hair and a short, well-trimmed beard. William Morris soon fell under his influence and, after obtaining his degree at Oxford, became a pupil of G. E. Street, one of the new Gothic revivalist architects who shared Morris's interest in church music and Flemish painting. His evenings were spent with his friends in violent discussions upon poetry, painting and the general arts and the launching in 1856 of a literary publication, the *Oxford and Cambridge Magazine*. Morris grew so interested in painting that, encouraged by Rossetti, he decided early in 1857 to become a painter. His ambition in this field outstripped his undoubted promise. It led to his meeting with other important figures, including the poet Algernon Charles Swinburne (1837–1909), who was

[1] Ruskin J. *The Seven Lamps of Architecture* New York, 1849

then a restless, red-haired romantic, and Philip Webb (1831–1915), a colleague in Street's studio. It was Webb who, in 1859, designed the Red House, Bexley-heath, Kent, for his friend Morris and his new wife, the dreamy-eyed Jane Burden, with her masses of dark, undulating hair. This new house was conceived by Morris in the style of the thirteenth century, and although the interior was much darker than is customary at the present time, it carried the imprint of a strong personality in its attempt to recreate the atmosphere of a medieval court with elaborate furnishings and decorations. Webb designed new furniture in a plain, heavy, Gothic fashion, simple table glass, candlesticks of copper, dressers for Morris's Dutch china, grates, fire-irons and a Gothic-style carriage for drives in the country. The ceilings and walls were decorated with partly completed painted patterns and murals, and embroidered hangings by the friends' wives and families. The windows were filled with allegorical stained glass designed by Burne-Jones and the floors covered with the richest of Persian carpets. Furniture was decorated with rich colours in medieval scenes. The lower drawing-room had a built-in settle with a minstrel gallery above, while the upper drawing-room possessed a ceiling painted with bands of foliage and wide stripes, and rising to a point like a tent.

Outside the house were creepers against the walls and a garden of rose-covered wattle fences, lilies, and the flower of the period, sunflowers.

The decoration and furnishing of this house over several years marked the culmination of Morris's development as the founder of the whole movement for a revival of taste in the mid-nineteenth century, to which Morris had linked a crusade for an improvement in social conditions.

He had found it impossible to buy any contemporary articles in what he felt was a good, honest, appropriate style. He and his friends, who now included the painter Ford Madox Brown (1821–93), who was also designing furniture and stained glass, had found it necessary to undertake most of the designing and making of all they required. At Brown's suggestion they considered combining to form a firm of art decorators. This association, with the advantage of Morris's wealth behind it and with good connections with the architectural profession, was established in April 1861 as 'Morris, Marshall, Faulkner and Company. Fine Art Workmen in Painting, Carving, Furniture and the Metals'. Charles Faulkner was a mathematician and a lifelong friend of Morris; Peter Marshall was a surveyor friend of Brown; other partners not mentioned in the title were Burne-Jones, Webb, Rossetti and Madox Brown.

It is against this background that the Great Exhibition must be considered. In 1756–7 the Society of Arts (now the Royal Society of Arts) sponsored in London a formal display of manufactured goods, offering prizes for specimens of manufactures, tapestry, porcelain, etc. This was followed by local exhibitions until 1847, when the Society was granted its Royal Charter and staged the first of a series of exhibitions of manufactures which stressed good design as a major consideration. The key men in this new emphasis were the Prince Consort, the President of the Society since 1843, and Henry Cole (1808–82), an official of the Public Record Office and a most vigorous innovator of new projects; he was later Controller of the South Kensington Museum, a forerunner of the present Victoria and Albert Museum. Cole had visited the exhibitions staged by the French Government in Paris and wished to promote similar but better ventures in this country. In 1847 he had founded a firm called Summerly's Art Manufactures with a view to persuading artists to design goods for manufacture.

The new annual exhibitions were outstanding successes, and in 1848 it was decided to hold, in 1851, a great National Quinquennial Exhibition, later changed to an International one. Despite bitter controversy over almost everything connected with this project, the whole vast plan finally came to fruition on 1 May 1851. *The Times*' leader next day stated: 'There was yesterday witnessed a sight the like of which has never happened before and which in the nature of things can never be repeated. They who were so fortunate as to see it hardly knew what most to admire, or in what form to clothe the sense of wonder and even of mystery which struggled within them. The edifice, the treasures of art collected therein, the assemblage and the solemnity of the occasion, all conspired to suggest something even more than sense could scan, or imagination attain. . . . Around them, amidst them, and over their heads were displayed all that is useful or beautiful in nature or in art . . . some saw . . . a solemn dedication of art and its stores; . . . there was so much that seemed accidental and yet had a meaning, that no one could be content with simply what he saw.'

This was not the view of William Morris or of Ruskin.[1] When Morris visited the Crystal Palace and the Great Exhibition of 1851 he vehemently declared that it was 'wonderfully ugly' and, sitting down, refused to walk around.[2] Even Henry Cole was bitter in his outspoken criticism of the articles on display. The ebb to harsh colours and crude realism was further accentuated between 1850 and 1870. Even the advice of such men as A. W. N. Pugin, the indefatigable advocate of Gothic forms, the architect Owen Jones, who also designed chintz, and Bruce J. Talbert (1838–81), a prolific designer strongly influenced by the Japanese, had not greatly affected the climate of opinion. Jones in 1863 wrote upon 'the demoralising influence of imitating Nature so directly as is the custom in the present day'. He was one of the first to attempt to abstract plant and flower forms rather than translating them into literal copies. Three levels of taste and appreciation are apparent during this period. The first was that of the majority of manufacturers and the general public, particularly the lower and lower-middle classes. Here the emphasis was on the cheapness and mass production possible with the new machinery, dyes and methods. The second was that of the group of men around Henry Cole, who believed that if the standards of design were raised, then this would result in a steady improvement in commercial production. This they felt could be achieved in part by encouraging artists to

[1] *The Works of John Ruskin* ed Cook E. T. and Wedderburn A. London, 1904 X, pp 193, 201
[2] Morris C. *Art Journal Easter Annual* 1899, p 1

...signs. The establishment of the Government Schools of Design was all part of this process (see plate 37).

The third level was that suggested by Ford Madox Brown when he proposed the formation of a firm of 'Art Decorators'. His innovation was the proposal that the artists should do more than design: they should take part in the production and sale of their designs. They should not hand over their inspiration to a factory and manager whose ideals would be inevitably shoddy, lacking in any form of inspiration, but dedicate their own lives to the crafts. Ruskin gave them support when he assaulted the accepted division of society into intellectuals or 'morbid thinkers' and manual or 'miserable workers'. '. . . It would be well if all of us were good handicraftsmen in some kind, and the dishonour of manual labour done away with altogether.'[1] These ideas he linked to the individuality and originality he saw in medieval life, qualities fostered again by the Gothic Revival of his time.

The new firm started in premises at 8 Red Lion Square, London, a few doors away from Morris's pre-Red House dwelling at No. 17, which he had shared with Burne-Jones from 1856 to 1859 and where the friends and others of their circle had first designed, made and decorated furniture, and planned frescoes for the University debating-hall at Oxford. These frescoes were carried through by the friends with so much more enthusiasm than technical ability or knowledge that they deteriorated within a short while. They did, however, introduce the young idealists to a practical situation and they profited from the experience in the new firm which soon became known as Morris and Company.

At first the prospectus stressed the need for artistic supervision and detailed co-operation in the execution of all forms of decorative work. The work produced was not cheap and catered in the main for architects who commissioned stained glass and wall and roof decorations for the new buildings they were designing. Morris was thorough in his own personal research into all the firm's increasing activities. By 1865 he had virtually assumed control of the firm which had moved, together with Morris and his family, to new and larger premises at 26 Queen Square, London. The new arrangement meant that Burne-Jones and Webb worked closely with Morris, who had to bolster up the annual deficits from his own pocket. Although stained glass dominated the output, by the late 1860s Morris had shown his outstanding skill as a designer, perhaps the greatest pattern designer of all time, in a limited number of naturalistic wallpapers produced by an outside firm during 1862–6. These did not sell at the time and Morris diverted much of his energy to poetry and prose, travel, the study of Icelandic sagas, and attempts to solve his relations with his wife, the 'dark, silent, medieval woman with her medieval toothache and strange, sad, deep, dark Swinburnian eyes', as Henry James described her.[2]

Improvements in the turnover of the firm initiated by a new manager, Warrington Taylor, in 1865, which involved a major change of policy in provid-

[1] Ruskin J. *The Seven Lamps of Architecture* New York, 1849
[2] *The Letters of Henry James* ed Lubbock P., 1920, 1, pp 17–19

ing a stock of goods rather than working only to commission, led Morris into new fields of design. He recommenced production of wallpapers in 1873, showing a still further mastery of his designs based on a fresh and individual use of natural sources. In the same year he started to experiment with printed textiles. Here he had so much difficulty in obtaining the clear, permanent colours he wanted for his first floral design in greens and yellows, Tulip and Willow, which he had sent to Thomas Clarkson of Bannister Hall to be printed, that he decided he must experiment for himself. To do this he sought the co-operation of Thomas Wardle of Leek, a recognized authority on silk cultivation and dyeing. It was readily given him, although at a financial loss to Wardle, and for two years Morris thoroughly explored the art of dyeing, studying techniques, working in the vats himself and gradually selecting those commercial dyes which were reliable, and reviving the almost obsolete indigo and madder vat dye methods. Until he had examined and practised many old vegetable recipes and forgotten methods he was not satisfied that he had produced a sufficiently large palette of unfading, clear, bright colours to carry out his designs. In 1876 he set up a dyehouse on a small scale at Queen Square, and taught the craft of dyeing, as he had taught so many crafts, to assistants. Until he was satisfied that they knew what to do and how to do it, he continued to experiment, and train his craftsmen (see plate 42).

At the same time, the increasing responsibility and work undertaken by Morris and the emphasis upon pattern designing for wallpapers and textiles brought about a crisis in the affairs of the firm. In 1875 the firm was officially reconstituted as Morris and Company and came under the sole control of Morris. The wrangles produced by this controversy caused a complete break with Rossetti, and a long period of estrangement from Madox Brown.

Once Morris was assured of the technical process, he started to design again, and by 1881 produced sixteen fabrics printed by Thomas Wardle, and a further twenty-eight printed in Morris's own print-works and weaving workshops established in 1881 at Merton Abbey, Surrey. Here he could directly supervise the whole process, including the indigo discharge process which he had wanted to use and which he felt beyond his previous printer's capabilities. This work continued until the eventual winding up of the firm in 1940, long after Morris's death (see plate 46).

Morris himself, once he had established the printed textile side of his multifarious activities, turned more and more to other interests. Although at first these included embroidered altar frontals and other cloths, embroidery designs for the Royal School of Needlework and other societies, and a continuation of hand-woven carpets and tapestries, he gradually re-entered the sphere of socialism that the Brotherhood had discussed so vehemently in the old days. The managing of his firm, his work in letterpress, his public lectures, writing, editing, poetry, advice to museums and libraries and his entry into politics all engaged more of his time. He wrote many books, among them *The Dream of John Ball* (1886–7) and *News from Nowhere* (1890). He founded the Kelmscott Press (1890) and with typical Morris thoroughness immersed himself in a new venture, designing type, borders and initial letters, and choosing ink and paper. His overwhelming drive burnt itself out and he died in October 1896.

His place in the firm was taken by his assistant, John Henry Dearle (1860–1932), who designed most of the new printed textiles they produced after 1900.

The development of Morris and his work with printed textiles have been covered at length because his was the first really conscious attempt to replace the hack designer and the commercial printer with a true union of artist-craftsman. Many similar movements appeared after Morris. His was the first and perhaps the most successful reaction against the often monotonous and shoddy productions of the machine. His designs, with superbly balanced colours, rich and well-controlled elaboration of pattern form and the contrast of fine, delicate drawing of natural things with bold, imaginatively placed shapes became so popular that Morris chintzes were the epitome of good design in both England and the United States. Since he first produced them, they seem to have existed alongside the fashions and trends that came and went with other textile designs.

In addition, his insistence on truth to material had considerable influence upon many architects and artists who became designers, such as C. F. A. Voysey (1857–1941), A. H. Mackmurdo (1851–1942), Walter Crane (1845–1915), Lewis F. Day (1845–1910), Philip Webb (1831–1915), Baillie Scott (1865–1945), C. R. Ashbee (1863–1942), C. R. Mackintosh (1868–1928), Norman Shaw (1831–1912), Christopher Dresser (1834–1904), Alan Vigers, Sydney Cockerell (1867–1962), W. R. Lethaby (1857–1931), W. A. S. Benson and Herbert Horne.

Morris was the leading member of the whole of the Arts and Crafts Movement of his time. This movement had arisen out of the Gothic Revival, but was now separate and proceeding on its own course. As distinct from a mere revival, this new movement was based upon the whole field of design. It was the first stirring of Basic Design.

Morris himself influenced many bodies such as the Century Guild founded by Mackmurdo, Selwyn Image (1849–1930), and Horne in 1882, which produced a number of interesting textiles printed by Simpson and Godlee of Manchester, as well as wallpaper and furniture. Its aim was 'to render all branches of art the sphere no longer of the tradesman but of the artist'.[1] Image wrote, 'Fine art is not the counterfeit of Nature'. In his style of design, Horne was a most interesting precursor of the work of the 1890s and of the Art Nouveau movement that stretched on to World War I.

The Art Furniture Alliance was formed by Christopher Dresser in 1880. Dresser had trained at the National School of Design and became famous for his work on three-dimensional design and the fundamentals of Japanese design. His Alliance had a showroom in London where many craft wares including textiles were sold (see plate 54).

[1] Century Guild *Aims and Intentions* 1882

Another now-famous store also became noted at this time. Liberty's was one of the first stores that commissioned designs directly from designers. To his stocks of imported goods, including work from Japan, Lazenby Liberty added many of the new fabrics and eventually set up his own printing establishment at Merton Abbey, near to that of Morris, and began the long series of printed textiles under the name of Liberty. On the Continent these designs were synonymous with Art Nouveau, and in Italy the *Stile Liberty* was the height of fashion. Among leading designers of textiles commissioned to produce the fabrics were Arthur Wilcock and Lindsay Butterfield in the 1890s, and Arthur Silver, who, as well as opening his own studio in 1880, designed a whole range of cheap fabrics for Liberty which brought these exciting designs within the reach of all (see plate 49).

Heywood Summer was one of the most interesting artist-designer decorators of the style. Others working independently in the field of printed textiles were Walter Crane, a prodigious designer of illustrated books and wallpapers, but also noted for his textile designs; Leon V. Solon (1872–1957), mainly a potter, but also designer of some textiles; Allan F. Vigers and Sidney Mawson who had great success around 1905 with delicate and naturalistic patterns in the popular bright, clear colours.

In 1884 The Home Arts and Industries Association was started with an interest in rural crafts.

C. R. Ashbee had also developed Morris's original ideas of socialism and the worth of craftsmanship in his Guild and School of Handicraft established in 1888, which helped to train, under rather medieval rules, a large number of craftsmen and designers.

The Art Workers' Guild, 1884, grew out of the Century Guild, a group of designers sponsored by Lewis F. Day called The Fifteen, and another group of artists and designers under the banner of St George's Art Society. The Guild was established as including 'Handicraftsmen and Designers in the Arts'. By 1888 it had become the Arts and Crafts Exhibition Society. This Society held exhibitions, encouraged discussion, sponsored lectures—Morris lectured to them several times upon textiles—and eventually led to the formation of the Central School of Arts and Crafts in 1894, under W. R. Lethaby as head, and to the gradual acceptance that designers could be trained to design for industry. It was insisted that this could only be done by practising the craft for which they wished to design. The Royal College of Art was also a great influence in this form of designing for industry, a function of the College that has been re-emphasized since the last war (see plate 47).

These movements were typically English and often extremely naïve. Yet, in the field of printed textiles, the influence of so many different approaches linked by the same basic philosophy not only rejuvenated the training of designers in this country but also played a part in the development of the crafts upon the Continent up to and including the Bauhaus in Germany, and also in France and Holland.

The work of Morris acted as a catalyst upon many differing designers and theorists. As a designer he was outstanding, and although the designs of his contemporaries often bear little relationship to his own, it is true to say that the great break with the traditional that occurred during the last three decades of the nineteenth century would not have been possible without the liberating thought and example given by Morris, who asked 'What business have we with art at all unless all can share it?'[1] His limitations lay in his looking backward, not forward, back to a form of society no longer practicable, back to a society without the machine.

Other designers, however, gradually abandoned these attitudes and C. R. Ashbee eventually wrote 'Modern civilization rests on machinery and no system . . . can be found that does not recognize this'.[2] Others who practised a great deal of textile design included Lewis F. Day: 'The public . . . want machine work . . . we may protest . . . but they will not pay much heed to us.'[3] Nevertheless, his designs and those of Herbert Horne, Christopher Dresser and C. F. A. Voysey, whilst under the influence of Morris looked forward to the mannerisms of Art Nouveau (see plate 48).

In textiles, this new and relatively short movement showed a strong drive towards mysticism, the Orient and especially Japan, and all that was 'strange, exotic, or quaint', words much in vogue in the movement. The printed fabrics showed the soft, organic curves, the elongated, outlined forms with a sense of growing structures derived in part from the Japanese prints of Hokusai, and in part from the strong design of William Blake. Walter Crane, the most popular of the disciples of William Morris, declared that this preoccupation with surface decoration was 'turning our artists into craftsmen and our craftsmen into artists'.[4] Art Nouveau was a direct descendant of the Arts and Crafts Movement and so of William Morris. Even at its peak it is possible to discern Morris's influence in the textiles of such designers as Mackmurdo, which were produced as early as 1882, although this work with its strange switches of rhythm between the bold pattern shapes and the delicately sinuous lines is distinctly Art Nouveau. Later he developed the ability to abstract from the natural source to such a degree that the new shapes could not be recognized and became liquid flames of oranges and dark reds moving organically over the fabric. Mackmurdo was probably the most daring Art Nouveau designer of textiles (see plates 50 and 56).

Others such as Ashbee and Voysey acted as a link or compromise between the looking back of Morris and the new twentieth century, although on the Continent they were considered as innovators of English Art Nouveau. This style, however, had been created in Britain during the eighties, although it was not accepted there as wholeheartedly as it was on the Continent. In textiles in

[1] Mackail J. W. *The Life of William Morris* 1899, reissued World Classics OUP 1950, p 99
[2] Ashbee C. R. *Should we stop teaching Art!* London, 1911, p 4; *Where the Great City Stands* London, 1917, p 3
[3] Day L. F. *Everyday Art; Short Essays on the Arts Not-Fine* London, 1882, pp 273–4
[4] Crane W. *National Association for the Advancement of Art and its Application to Industry, Transactions Liverpool Meeting, 1888* London, p 216

England the transition from the recreated historicism of Morris through the Arts and Crafts Movement to the conformity with all organic structure of Art Nouveau, and thence to the Modern Movement, proceeded without the deliberate break with tradition so evident in the rest of Europe. Voysey in particular had, by 1908, refined his earlier use of nature as a source for his textile designs from large, papery poppies, twisting leaves and stylized buds, to simplified, decorative, almost linear patterns on plain backgrounds that expressed his desire to 'live and work in the present'. This was very different from the controlled crowding of Morris in the 1870s, or even the more simplified arrangements of the 1890s. So, too, were the approaches of Christopher Dresser (1834–1904) in his later designs, Harry Napper (d. 1930) and Frank Brangwyn (1867–1956), who produced a number of outstanding but neglected textile designs during this period. A fashion for Oriental designs printed on black grounds lasted from 1910 to 1920 and a number of roller-printed fabrics were designed by such artists as Eric Howard for William Foxton. At the same period, Charles Shannon RA, Claude Lovat-Fraser, Albert Griffiths and Sidney Haward all designed block and roller prints and also designed cretonnes for Foxton, Turnbull and Stockdale, and other firms (see plates 44, 55 and 61).

Around the 1920s the Scottish architect and designer Charles Rennie Mackintosh designed a number of textiles in the highly individual manner he had employed in decorative features of the Glasgow School of Art Library, for which he was architect from 1907 to 1910. Mackintosh was one of the geniuses of the whole group of Art Nouveau designers. His concept of architecture was not limited to the building, but also included the furnishings and decoration. His work was shown throughout Europe and caused much interest and excitement in its treatment of the function and the geometry of architectural space. His textile designs show undulating forms which, with more violent colours, became insistent in his later work. His wife Margaret, and her sister Frances McDonald, also designed fabrics, and this rather delayed extension of the Art Nouveau movement formed part of the whole Glasgow movement in architecture and design (see plate 59).

It was not until Roger Fry (1866–1934) started his Omega workshops in 1913 with Vanessa Bell, Frederick Etchells and Duncan Grant, and later Wyndham Lewis, Gaudier-Brzeska, Henri Doucet and Nina Hamnet, that the studio craftsman-artist combination again appears. It opened at premises in Fitzroy Square, London, and employed young painters at 30s a week for part-time work designing and decorating. Here a group of artists 'sought delight in creation in the making of objects for common life'[1] to keep 'the spontaneous freshness of primitive or peasant work while satisfying the needs . . . of the modern, cultivated man'.[2] The workshops produced furniture, pottery, carpets, stained glass, complete schemes for interior decoration and fine printed textiles. The group lasted until June 1919, but unfortunately its activities and immediate impact

[1] Fry R. *Omega, A Statement of Intention* 1913
[2] *The Studio* i, 1893, p 234

were disrupted by the Great War. The work, which was produced anonymously under an Ω as a signature, provoked a great deal of interest in the Press and with the general public. This 'Post-Impressionist Manner' of furnishing a house, as it became known, was often ridiculed as very advanced design and not recognized as so much better than the general level of household articles at that time. Fry, with his native Puritanism, his brilliant career at Cambridge, his interests in the art of Japan and eighteenth-century France and the life aesthetic, his extensive travels and experience as an adviser to the millionaire buyer Pierpont Morgan and the Metropolitan Museum, brought an air of refinement and a knowledge of current European movements in art and design, and particularly of the genius of Cézanne, to the doctrine of Art for Art's sake. 'It might even be', he wrote, 'that we should . . . justify nature by its likeness to art.' It was these arbiters of taste, the Bloomsbury set, and the Omega workshops that reintroduced a sense of design in depth or pure form, by basing their textile designs in particular upon a version of Cubism. At this distance in time it is possible to see the approach of the dilettante thinker in some of their work. Additionally the movement drew attention to young designers and gave them practical work and encouragement at a time when grants from industry and organizations were very restrictive (see plate 60).

After the war the fashion for geometric and abstract design set by the Omega workshops was led by the firms of W. Foxton Ltd, and F. W. Grafton, and much influenced by the then current vogue of the Russian ballet towards the strong colours of purple and orange with thick black outlines. These crude colourings became most popular, and many artist-designers connected with the Arts and Crafts Exhibition Society began producing their own textiles around 1923. They often reverted to the use of wood blocks which they designed, cut and printed themselves, using vegetable dyes in low, dark tones and making extensive use of the discharge and resist techniques that had fallen into disuse since Morris's own experiments.

Amongst them were two pioneer printed-textile craftsmen, Phyllis Barron (1890–1964), and her friend and partner Dorothy Larcher. Barron had studied drawing and painting at the Slade School, and while there had been given some old French textile-printing blocks. She found such difficulty in obtaining advice on how to use them that before and during the Great War, with the help of Bancroft's *Philosophy of Permanent Colours* (1813) and other old books, she rediscovered nitric acid discharges on indigo-red cloth, how to print with iron liquor or acetate of iron on cloth mordanted with powdered oak galls, how to print with cutch and similar long-forgotten recipes (see plate 66).

Her work was shown in the displays of the Omega workshops although she declined Fry's invitation to join the group. If she had done so, her instinctive feeling for design and the practical knowledge she had acquired of printing and dyeing might have provided the group with the necessary practicality that their textile work so often seems to miss. She was joined by the painter Dorothy Larcher in 1923 and from then until the Second World War they produced a vast output of printed cottons, linens and silks from their house in Painswick, where they established their workshop in 1930. These textiles had a great influence upon other designers. They have a peculiarly English quality of rest and timelessness such as is apparent in many of the chintz designs by William Morris.

Barron often said that she felt Morris was far too 'industrially minded'. She was one of the great craftsmen designers who appeared between the world wars, others being such persons as Ethel Mairet, the dyer, spinner and weaver, and Bernard Leach, the potter. Although Barron took no pupils as such she influenced other persons and particularly Susan Bosence, who worked with her in Mrs Bosence's workshop at Yarner in South Devon during the 1950s. In 1960 she was joined by Annette Kok and during a most successful five-year partnership produced many lengths of wax and paste resists and small print designs. They now carry on their work as members of the staff of the Devon Centre for Further Education as well as continuing to print textiles in their own workshops. Mrs Bosence points out that 'whereas Phyllis Barron in her heyday could afford to employ four printers from among the village girls such a staff would, nowadays, cost a fortune, since they can earn fantastic sums in local factories. If you want to keep up your standards, and we are uncompromising idealists, then you have to do the work yourself.'

A number of other hand fabric printers have worked in this country since World War II, including Margaret Holgate at Oakridge Lynch, Gloucestershire, and The Mill House Printers, Penzance, Cornwall. The early 1920s showed a revival in this country, and more so in America, in the batik process, and a number of firms and particularly F. W. Grafton & Co, Manchester, produced similar effects by machine printing (see plate 43).

In the early 1930s there was a fashion among commercial designers for muted colours and pastel shades, as was shown in the designs of Mea Angerer for Eton Rural Fabrics, Constance Irving for W. Foxton Ltd, and Frank Ormrod for Turnbull and Stockdale Ltd.

Other designers who produced a great deal of work for Foxton were Minnie McLeish and Gregory Brown (see plate 62).

The Paris Exhibition of 1925 brought in an even greater emphasis upon geometric formalization and, as Bevis Hillier points out in *Art Deco*, produced an antithesis to its progenitor Art Nouveau. Not only Cubism and the Russian Ballet, but also ancient Egyptian art, the Bauhaus and the design of Aztec temples all contributed to the development of Art Deco. This reached a culmination in the Odeon or Cinema style of architecture and the applied arts in the 1930s (see plate 64).

In the printed textiles of Art Deco we find two forms of design emerging; the earlier is shown by the iridescent bubble patterns of E. O. Hoppé, a reaction against the directness of Cubism, and the later by the McKnight Kauffer interpretation of aggressive Cubism in, for example, the work of H. and M. Farman. This phase in the 1930s brought dynamism and strong vigorous patterns symbolic of youth and the *Herrenvolk*. To the exponents of the artistic creeds of

41

this time, the Morris and Japanese principle of 'truth to material' was no longer valid. Design became applied design, and often showed little relationship to the thickness, quality or function of the fabric to which it was applied. Only a few textile craftsmen, among whom were Barron, Larcher, Enid Marx and Jane Edgar, did not subscribe in some way to this style.

Within the style were the brilliantly patterned textiles by Gunta Stölzl and Sonia Delauney-Terk.

Screen printing

In the 1930s this new method of printing came into general use and quickly supplanted all other forms, at first in the middle and upper price ranges, and by the 1950s, in all ranges.

In principle, screen printing is essentially the same as stencilling. It was in Japan that the printing of cotton and crêpe fabrics with stencils was first practised, during the second half of the seventeenth century. Its invention is attributed to a Shinto priest called Yuzen and it is by this name that the method is known today. The stencils are cut from board, very tough paper or thin metal sheets. Because of the difficulty with floating parts in the centre of some shapes, these parts were trapped in place with untwisted silk thread or a network of human hair. The card or paper was soaked in oil or varnish to make it waterproof. The dye was applied with a brush or pad. In time, the hairs were fixed across a wooden frame, and later a silk gauze was used, and so the silk screen as we know it came into use. Some of the early Yuzen prints employed more than a hundred separate stencils and as many colours in the printing of one kimono. The squeegee employed to force the dye through the parts of the silk screen not blocked out with varnish or other stopper was a much later invention (see plate 86).

F. W. Mackenzie, in the *Journal of the Society of Dyers and Colourists* (p 196) 1938, states that the Polygraphia Society reproduced old masters between 1830 and 1840 by what was probably a screen printing method. The method fell into disuse due to the rise in the use of lithography for printing pictures.

As far as is known, the technique was not used in Europe as screen printing on cloth until well into the nineteenth century, when the first *imprimés à la Lyonnaise* were produced on silk at Lyons. Because of their great cost, these found a small, exclusive but ready market, and the process spread, on a limited basis, to Switzerland and Germany. The method was not generally accepted until the experiments in the United States at the beginning of this century showed the economic possibilities.

The first patent for a screen printing process was taken out by Samuel Simon of Manchester in 1907 and John Pilsworth used the method in 1915 to produce banners for the U.S. Army. Further patents showed improved methods with photographic screens (1915 and 1921), carbon tissue stencil screens (1920), a silk screen printing press (1921), a silk screen stencilling press for textiles (1925) and the stencil film process (1930). The first commercial screen printing on fabric in bulk is thought to have started in France in 1926. By the 1930s screen printing works had been established in many parts of Europe and the United States; the technique revolutionized first the furnishing textile trade and then, as screens and dyes were improved, the dress fabric market.

Whereas printing with engraved rollers and hand blocks had been laborious and costly in all the stages of preparation and printing, the silk screen greatly increased the freedom of the designer, and allowed the manufacturer to try out limited editions of textiles without tying up large capital sums in expensive rollers and blocks. Screens are relatively easy and cheap to produce and allow any type of design to be reproduced exactly to the smallest detail.

In the 1930s succeeding recessions caused a shrinkage of markets. At the same time, the designs lost touch with the wishes of the non avant-garde. As the demand for a design fell less yardage was sold, and because of high initial costs the manufacturers' price per yard increased, and the spiral repeated itself in still lower sales and higher prices. To avoid the wholesale bankruptcy resulting from shrinking markets and excessive costs it was imperative to find a cheaper method. Screen printing provided the manufacturer with one during a difficult period, and when the economy improved the lessons learnt were carried on in the new situation of more rapidly changing fashions.

Some of the first manufacturers to use this process on a large basis were Allan Walton Textiles, Calico Printers Association Ltd, Donald Brothers, Edinburgh Weavers and the Old Bleach Linen Company. Well-known artists designing for them were Duncan Grant, Vanessa Bell, Paul Nash (1889–1946), Hans Tisdall, Marion Dorn, Michael O'Connell and Ben Nicholson (b. 1894).

Other processes developed during the nineteenth century

(A number of these methods are treated in more detail in *A History of Dyed Textiles* by the same author)

Apart from the printing *on a fabric* techniques textile printers have always shown great interest in the methods of resisting or discharging dye. The traditional methods of starch and wax resist by hand application with a brush or *tjanting* were too laborious and time-consuming for the commercial printer in Europe to employ. On the other hand, such fabrics possessed a brilliance of colour and charm of accidental effects (such as the crackle of wax batik) which made them very appealing to the consumer. Europeans and Japanese explored a number of allied techniques among which were the following.

The Golgas Method first used by a German printer in Normandy in 1762 and extensively used until the 1850s. It employed identical matching engraved wooden boards to dye flannel under pressure with a variety of colours at once. Each colour had its own channels in which to run. The method gave a blurred outline and would seem to be based on an original Chinese technique introduced into Japan in the sixth century and known as *Kyo-kechi*.

The Beryll or Berill Method was probably of English origin and was extensively used in Normandy by one Jacques de Marcis around 1729. The method involved deeply engraved brass plates. The design was filled with thickened colour and the surface wiped clean. The brass plate was placed on an iron plate that could be heated. The woollen cloth to be printed was put on the engraved brass plate, the whole being packed over with a heavy woollen cover which was kept wet. All was then placed in a press. The great heat of the iron plate together with the steam from the woollen cover not only fixed the colour but also crimped the printed cloth to give an embossed effect. Excess colour or thickener was carefully brushed off and the result was excellent apart from the fact that it could not be washed.

The Brahma Press Method was invented by a Glasgow printer, Monteith, around 1810. The following notes, supplied by the Dyestuffs Division, I.C.I. Ltd, Manchester, give very interesting accounts of how the Brahma techniques were practised.

It is unlikely that liquid chlorine as such was used. A solution of a hypochlorite appears much more likely. The fact that acid hypochlorites were needed is frequently stated in relation to the bleaching of dyed Turkey reds.

Practical Treatise on Dyeing & Callicoe Printing by T. Cooper (Professor of Chemistry in Dickenson College, Carlisle, Pennsylvania) Philadelphia 1815 p 423. 'A method of printing spots, or rather producing spots by a discharging liquor on Bandana handkerchiefs, has lately been introduced. A partial account of this process is given under the article 'discharging' in the new edition of Rees' cyclopaedia, but as I cannot find the plate of the machinery published as yet, instead of copying the article I shall only refer to it. The principle is to apply a paste of oxymuriat [*sic*] of lime to the spot to be discharged, to decompose the oxymuriat by means of sulphuric acid and to confine the operation by means of a screw press precisely within the bounds of the pattern. This process might be applied to blues and supersede paste work, and also to patterns on yellow grounds. In fact, as the invention is new as yet, we cannot see all the purposes to which it can be extended. It occurs to me at present that the following method not hitherto used or suggested might be employed for the same general purpose.

'Let the pattern be stamped out on two corresponding plates of sheet lead of any dimensions. Smear the lead with paste, both the upper and under plates. Fix the cloth between. Apply force or pressure, if necessary, to keep them together. Enclose them in a box or a room and throw in oxymuriatric or chlorine gas for a short time. If needful the cloth might be moistened to prevent the corrosive effect of the acid.

'In the same way a dyed piece of any colour might be discharged in patterns, by printing on it a blotch ground in paste work or reserve and exposing the open work moistened to oxymuriatic acid. These ideas have never been suggested or practised that I know of, but I am satisfied they are feasible from the experiments on chlorine gas which I usually introduce in my chemical lectures before the class.'

Bleaching and Calico Printing: A Practical Manual, G. Duerr and W. Turnbull. Published Griffin & Co London 1896. No mention of presses. Turkey red discharges obtained by passing into a soaper containing hypochlorite fabric printed with acids are described.

Practical and Theoretical Treatise on the Printing of Textiles by J. Persoz. Published Paris, V. Masson 1846 (Vol. 3) (in French) p 232 para. No. 624. 'Discharging with chlorine: This process was first developed in England particularly for the printing of Turkey red. It appears to have been known already for some time for we found in some unedited notes of M. Daniel Koechlin (1811) that a Scot had already before this epoch printed handkerchiefs on a sort of Turkey red . . .'

A practical handbook of dyeing and calico printing by W. Crookes FRS. Published Longmans London 1874 p 317. '. . . The process generally known as Monteith's consists in the direct application of a solution of chlorine to the dyed fabrics. (Note that Persoz, while stating that Monteith had operated the style successfully from 1818, acknowledges that a Scot had operated the style even before 1811.) The Turkey red dyed fabrics are placed in folds properly smoothed and arranged between two thick cast lead plates, both of which are perforated with the design to be produced, the perforations exactly corresponding; the cloth is then pressed between these plates with considerable force, and the plates secured. By this mechanical contrivance the wetting of the portions of the cloth tightly pressed between the unperforated parts of the plates is very effectually prevented, while any liquid poured on the upper plate will gradually filter through the cloth from the perforation to the corresponding one on the other. The passage of the discharging fluid (bleaching powder with an excess of free acid) is assisted by currents of air. When the colour is discharged clear water is passed through and the pieces then washed and finished. *As might be expected from the nature of the process, the edges of the design are not sharp and clear, because, notwithstanding any practical amount of pressure, capillary attraction will assert itself, and consequently the edges of the designs are blurred.*

'The other process frequently used for this purpose is the discovery of M. D. Koechlin and Mr Thompson. It consists in printing a highly acid paste upon the cloth to be discharged and then plunging it into a solution of bleaching powder in water; the acid acts upon the bleaching powder causing a disengagement of chlorine, which destroys the colour upon the spot where the acid is printed . . . Besides producing a white design, there are discharges which, whilst destroying the red colour, leave another in its place, or the basis for producing another.'

The Brahma process is also fully covered under the title of 'Machine Stencilling' in D. G. Kale's excellent *Principles of Cotton Printing* (Bombay) 1957 p 27.

The Discharge Methods were known in early times as a difficult technique which could easily 'tender' or rot the fabric if the chemicals used were too concentrated. To this day children will paint or print lemon juice upon a mild permanganate of potash dyed fabric to produce a discharged pattern. Not, I must add, the fastest of dyes, but quite suitable for primary school experiments. As an accepted commercial technique, using a roller, block or screen printed paste containing an oxidizing or reducing agent (such as the well-known brand of sodium sulphoxylate formaldehyde known as 'Formosul'), to remove a dischargeable dye from part of a dyed fabric, it has many advantages. The main one is the absence of join marks where a background is printed from a block or flat screen.

Although certain tribes, including the Bambara of French West Africa, employed mud containing metal salts both to fix a tannin brown on to a fabric and also to react with a mordant soap pattern previously applied to bleach out the tannin brown and leave a light pattern, the technique, as far as is known, was not extensively used until early in the nineteenth century. Amongst the experiments were those of Daniel Koechlin-Schouch (1785–1871), a prominent dyer in Mulhouse, Alsace. In this region a great deal of Turkey red was used in dyeing and Koechlin wished to find a method of discharging the red ground colour which would allow him to print other colours in their true shade on the discharged areas. He not only discovered that free hypochlorous acid bleached out the Turkey red to white and did not harm the fibre but that tartaric acid, Prussian blue and chloride of lime removed the Turkey red and left a blue in its place. By omitting the tartaric acid, he obtained black. These outstanding discoveries revolutionized textile decoration and in conjunction with the Kashmir pattern, so much in demand at this time, led to the production of Merinos or European imitations of Indian shawls in 1810.

Swiss factories and particularly those in the canton of Glarus took up the method and later it was adapted to the Perrotine machine (1865). Before then the technique had spread to England. It was used both as a normal method of printing and also for the production of the special fabrics known as Africa prints or Manchester batiks. Cloth was dyed with indigo or a synthetic dye and then patterns bleached out, so that further colours applied on top could fall on the bleached-out areas. With a knowledge and skilful use of dischargeable and non-dischargeable dyes, either mixed for piece dyeing and subsequent discharged, or a non-dischargeable dye print with the discharge paste on to a dischargeable ground shade, many complicated designs were produced. Other forms involved the printing of wax patterns and other resist pastes. The latter pastes may, of course, contain 'non-resistible' dyes.

The Batik or Resist Methods applicable to the printer of textiles employed either wax or starch pastes printed from a block to act as a resist to future dyeing processes. The original Indian and Javanese hand methods did not produce

46

enough fabrics to satisfy the wider and cheaper markets and the block known as a *tjap* was introduced from India into the Indonesian workshops. Since it was difficult to obtain full penetration of dye by one-side printing, each side had to be printed with a matching print. Not an easy technique with hot wax. Variations included the *Rô Kechi* method in Japan employing the application of liquid wax through fine wood stencils or heated wood blocks cut to simple 'hole' designs. Gold and silver metallic pastes in fine 'leaf' form were often applied from blocks in India and the surrounding areas.

The Indian and Indonesian blocks consisted of copper strips soldered together and inserted in a block of wood to form a shape of the required design. Using a handle attached to the back of the block, the *tjap* printer pressed the front of the block upon a piece of cloth, saturated with hot wax, in a shallow metal pan with legs, standing over a charcoal fire. Both sides were printed to match. In parts of southern India a clay paste compounded of a sticky clay, gum, crude sugar and water is block printed on the fabric to act as a resist before it is put in an indigo vat. This form of indigo resist printing was brought to Holland in the first place by the painter Pieter Coeck Van Aelst (father-in-law of Pieter Brueghel the Elder) after his travels in the East in the early sixteenth century. As other travellers returned with samples of fabrics and the Chinese blue-decorated porcelain a great interest in blue and white decoration was aroused. Since both indigo and cotton were imported the new technique of printing dispensed with the stiffening resulting from oil-bound pigment dyes and gave a result comparable with other techniques. It became variously known as the Dutch Method, the Swiss or Aquarel Method, as Porcelain printing, and sometimes as a version of Oberkampf's *toiles de Jouy* or *indiennes*. At the turn of the eighteenth century versions with additional block printing in a large number of colours were called lapis articles and later Perrotines from the machine invented in 1835 by a French engineer Louis-Jerome Perrot which printed six hundred yards of fabric in four colours in twelve hours and gave excellent imitations of hand printing.

The method spread quickly to parts of Germany where it evolved in Westphalia into a specialized form known as *Blaudruck*. A recipe of 1780 gives a resist with pipe clay and turpentine as the main ingredients printed from pear-wood blocks upon linen. The sticky impressions were later sprinkled with sand. When dry it was dipped in a warm blue dye and eventually the resist was washed out. Early patterns represented religious motifs, but in the nineteenth century these gave way to smaller units based on natural forms in stripes and all-over patterns. The cold method of indigo dyeing gradually superseded that of the older warm dyes. The blocks were also sometimes embellished with brass pins and strips driven in to them. The cloth went through the same process of preparation as for wax batik: it was washed, sized, and mangled (the equivalent of beating); spread on a padded table, block printed with the resist and dried; steeped in a dye vat using a block and pulley winch, cleaned off in an acid or mild vitriol bath and rinsed: it was finally dried and smoothed on a sleeking-board with a special kind of stone.

47

Slovakia is thought to have learned the secrets of Holland by way of Silesia, and textile printing is known to have been practised there by the end of the eighteenth century. A considerable industry developed with guilds, substantial export and home markets, a well-organized trade with pattern books, woodcut-illustrated broadsheets and many varieties of method, from hand blocks using carved wood or with metal strips, wedges and pins, to factory-made wire patterns printed by machine.

The reserve used in Slovakia consists of painters' white clay, gum Arabic, acetate of lead, lead sulphate, blue stone, salve, alum and water. The process is as already described.

Since the Slovak dyers live in the midst of a rural community, the patterns are still a reflection of the traditional way of life.

The Negative Reserve Methods involving the printing of mordants on the cloth and the subsequent dyeing one colour have already been referred to. There is one further very specialized form usually classed as a 'burnt out' style that has long been popular in India. The Dyestuffs Division, I.C.I. Ltd, Manchester, give the following information:

'We do know that in Ahmedabad, India, in the mid-1950s a style was operated along the following lines. Block print an outline with Calatac VA (ICI). Within the outline where it was desired to destroy the cotton, a thickened paste of ammonium sulphate or ammonium chloride would be printed. After hard drying or baking the cloth would be brushed to remove the degraded fibre. Calatac VA would be hardened by baking and to stop fraying around the printed areas. This had replaced a much older technique in which less satisfactory binders than Calatac VA were used. Naturally, if required, pigments could be incorporated in the Calatac VA just as in earlier binders (which were often egg or blood albumen-based).'

Textile design from 1939 to the present day

From 1939 to 1948 the war and its immediate aftermath restricted the output of both manufacturers and designers. Alastair Morton designed for Edinburgh Weavers, Josephine Cheeseman for Donald Brothers, Margaret Simeon for Allan Walton Textiles, Jacqueline Groag for Hill Brown Ltd and F. W. Grafton. It was, however, a difficult period for all types of textile printing. The necessities of the war had prevented the normal improvements in production techniques customary in what might have been a flourishing market. The designs often appear nondescript, as if the designers were marking time, and it was not until 1947 that the industry caught up with the new machinery available and began again the practice of commissioning designs from leading painters and sculptors.

Zika Ascher, of Ascher (London) Ltd, had always been interested in commissioning designs from famous artists. Henry Moore, whose work as a fabric designer he had seen at an exhibition arranged by the Cotton Board, designed a large reclining figure wall hanging for Ascher in 1944. This was followed by various exhibitions of designs for Ascher by Henri Matisse, André Derain, Cecil Beaton, Jean Cocteau, Robert Colquhoun, Lucien Freud, Barbara Hepworth, Ivor Hitchins, Francis Hodgkins, Jean Hugo, Marie Laurencin, Ben Nicholson, Francis Picabia, John Piper, Graham Sutherland, Feliks Topolski, Julian Trevelyan, John Tunnard and Keith Vaughan. Scarves and wall hangings posed a number of problems to designers, one of which Keith Vaughan described as 'to get a design which looks right in a rigid square', and 'which will hold together when the scarf becomes fluid' and the material is draped[1] (see plate 69).

In 1953, the *Ambassador* magazine held a similar exhibition 'Paintings into Textiles', at the Institute of Contemporary Arts at which leading painters and sculptors exhibited designs for textiles. Both Henry Moore for David Whitehead Ltd and William Gear for Edinburgh Weavers Ltd showed screen-printed fabrics.

Other painters also worked on printed textiles during the 1950s, such as John Piper for David Whitehead Ltd (1956), Hans Tisdall (1957) and Alan Reynolds (1959) for Edinburgh Weavers Ltd.

A new dimension in design and colour was caused by the impact upon the market of a whole range of printed textiles from the Lancashire firm of David Whitehead Ltd. Their designers included Roger Nicholson, Jacqueline Groag, T. Mellor, J. Feldman and M. Maller, as well as those from their own studio. These designs of small differing units in a wide range of bright colourways, printed on rayon or cotton, revolutionized the printed-textile industry of this period. It was also the beginning of the breakdown of the separation of furnishing and dress fabrics. Many of the Whitehead designs were used by home dressmakers whose numbers had been swollen by the increasing availability of new and much improved sewing machines, classes in institutes and colleges, magazine features on home dressmaking as well as the simpler styles now being accepted in the fashion world. This so-called contemporary style of enclosing motifs in square panels was a prevalent feature of the work of a number of designers and firms in the postwar period, including Jane Edgar for Heal and Son Ltd, Lucienne Day and Humphrey Spender for Edinburgh Weavers, Victoria Norrington and George Willis for Liberty and Co Ltd (see plate 67).

Trends of fashion were as prevalent as the modes of the nineties or crazes of the twenties. One of the first of these was the attempt in the immediate postwar years to continue the feeling of historical solidity and classical renaissance felt during the war. Screen prints appeared with stylized patterns based upon Greek mythology; Cretan urn motifs; the signing of the Magna Charta; running, jumping, galloping or any kind of horses; the Bayeux tapestry; the silver wedding of George VI and Queen Elizabeth in 1948 and similar themes. The

[1] Vaughan K. *Illustrated London News* 16 December 1966, p 32

Festival of Britain in 1951 and the Coronation of 1953 directly or indirectly inspired further loyal designs. Although intended for the West African and other markets, these were honestly royal and included many coloured and large repeats of the Queen and Prince Philip seated upon the coronation throne and surrounded by orbs, crowns, royal cyphers and other paraphernalia printed upon cotton dress fabric. The designs for the mass home market were a little more subtle in their association and relied upon roses, writhing-line decoration (reminiscent of cyphers), small medallion repeats containing a wide variety of pattern units.

This excursion down memory lane was so fully exploited by souvenir manufacturers that it was a relief when the clear bright colours, unusual tonal contrasts and angled geometric shapes of Scandinavian design suddenly swept the market with vivid textiles, stainless steel table and kitchen ware and clean, unusually shaped glass and pottery. This new approach to pure colour has persisted through each of the succeeding trends (see plates 81 and 85).

A reversion to textural prints and a greater use of brown and black followed, with the emphasis on a general deep tone quality which led to the short intrusion of a nostalgic thirties Hollywood look, an architectural attempt, a geometrical effect after Mondrian, a sortie to Pop prints and then settled into Op Art. The use of this painting form was helped by the ease with which basic design could be translated into a regular repeat upon dress or furnishing fabrics. The restriction to, in the main, black and white, or a deep tone on a lighter was not universally popular. It was obvious that these early attempts to popularize Bauhaus teaching were not accepted by a public only just up to Impressionism as an art form, and many yards were sold off in sales once the avant-garde had tired of the trend.

At this time two interesting ideas were introduced by Arthur Sanderson and Co. One was the identical matching of fabrics and a wallpaper, known as their Triad range, and later extended to include a further matching plain fabric to make a complementary set of a wallpaper, a printed and a plain textile. This idea originated in France and has been greatly developed in America.

The second was the reissue by Sandersons of a number of designs based on the original William Morris textiles with slightly adapted colours and pattern widths. These formed a wide and selective part of a Morris revival with exhibitions of his other activities.

This preceded a new trend that became most popular after the mid-1960s with the commercial revival of Art Nouveau, the meteoric rise of the Beatles, the growth of Carnaby Street, Gear, Habitat and similar stores. Art Nouveau fabrics were most popular and although they often bore little relation to the original inspiration did permit a great freeing of design from formal repetition.

When the Beatles sought the advice of an Indian mystic, textiles with an Oriental inspiration and Art Nouveau overtones were speedily upon the market. Such fabrics were popular with people who were sympathetic towards but not necessarily willing to be completely identified with the Flower People, who also provided the incentive for a short-lived vogue for dresses with one large flower, dragon, seedhead or other unit, screen printed on the back, front or both sides of the dress or tunic (see plate 83).

The quick turnover of fashion rapidly brought the Art Nouveau period of design through a short Jazz era in 1967, which hardly made an impact upon the public, to Art Deco and a revival of interest in 'the glittering twenties and thirties, the fabulous era of the Hollywood Spectacular and the yards of gold lamé and tasselled beads'.[1] So runs a handout of early 1968 and again, textiles, with the vulgar clichés of the twenties and thirties, the effects of changing lights in the mighty Würlitzer, the overtones of Egyptian architecture and the thousand and one Technicolor sunsets reflecting in the inevitable raindrops along Sunset Boulevard, appeared in reduced tones of mauve, green, orange and pink, all helped by the popularity of the film *Bonnie and Clyde*. Mexican and other South American sources provided the inspiration for a minor trend in the late 1968 season (see plates 76 and 78).

The ever-increasing and instant availability of the silk-screened fabric has meant that a large number of varied styles and colours can now be produced and, although one mode is dominant at one particular time, the many Top Tens of the textile world allow individual interpretation to switch from one trend to another, or even follow several at the same time. The old régime of a few fashion shows setting each year's styles has become outdated (see plate 84).

Art Deco as a genuine mass-culture development was linked with Pop Art and in the 1969–70 season, a number of printed textiles appeared with the Roy Lichtenstein trade marks in evidence. This serious attempt to utilize cartoon sources was at its most successful when parts of the source were employed as, for example, balloon shapes, dot-dash texture, swirling link lines with emphasis between thicks and thins and strong tonal contrasts. With this went a Peasant or Folk Art inspired movement among designers, evident in a number of textiles including Pat Albeck's Angel Pavement for Sanderson's. In mid-1969, an attempt was made to switch the trend to 'the baroque, the tapestry and the Oriental, eye-filling, sinuously swirling designs, sometimes derived from nature, sometimes Paisley with-a-difference and sometimes more geometric in inspiration'.[2] Occasionally, we find a combination of the three. The observer has the feeling that he has seen this film before, or perhaps only the trailer for it.

The new technical advances enabled textile designers to work without restriction, and any type of design could be faithfully reproduced. This freedom had its own inherent dangers. Morris believed in the need for a pattern to be indivisible from the textile upon which it was placed. Art, he believed, must not be the mere application of an unrelated design applied to a surface. There must be a total relationship between the design and the fabric. The ease and convenience of screen printing enabled textile decoration to copy exactly all other techniques. A photographically prepared screen could as easily reproduce patterns originally made by other processes such as batik, tie-dye, block and roller prints, as it could

[1] Sanderson Leaflet 1968/9
[2] Sanderson Leaflet 1968/9

copy brush or line drawings, photographs and any other graphic work. Only a few designers endeavoured to use the medium as one in its own right, and not as a reproductive tool. The tendency in art colleges has been away from the study of the traditional crafts and natural fibres so that they are becoming colleges which study art and design. This tendency, together with the increasing use of synthetic fibres, has led to many designs that appear to be enlargements of abstract or pictorial book illustration and other graphic work. In the 1960s particularly, the evident limitations of synthetic fibres in decorative textiles were in part overcome by the use of mixture fabrics such as cotton and terylene, wool and acrylic and other blends. It was obvious that the earliest synthetic fibres, whether regenerated or true synthetics, had grave technical disadvantages in use. As these factors, such as poor draping, non-absorption, yellowing, attractiveness to dirt, were entirely or partly eliminated, the resulting fabric, although much improved in performance, sometimes became bland and lifeless. This lack of character was accentuated when designs were placed upon the fabric background, and for some time the fabric was treated as a smooth canvas on to which a painted design, often indistinguishable from contemporary art, was applied (see plate 77).

The sudden strides in the dye chemistry relating to synthetic materials; the ability to obtain exceedingly brilliant and outstandingly fast colours; the recent developments in finishes including minimum-iron, easy stain release, drip dry, silicone treatment, permanently shrunk, permanently pleated, rinse wash, tumble dry and deodorant treatments (only some of a great number of applied finishes); and technical processes such as bonding in place of sewing—all these have played a major part in the new freedom of the designer.

Because screens could carry much larger designs than rollers, a fashion developed in the early 1960s for large-scale floral design. This was followed by abstract 'constructions', loosely derived from the basic design and foundation courses that mushroomed in colleges of art all over the country at that time. The revival of interest in the teachings of the Bauhaus also influenced designers and what can only be described as paintings upon cloth in 5 or 6 ft repeats appeared on the market. This particular aspect of screen printing is comparable with the fashion for souvenir handkerchiefs of the late eighteenth and nineteenth centuries. The short gap now possible between the planning of a new fashion, the preparation of the screens and full-scale appearance upon the market has made possible repeated changes in fashion which are no longer hampered by the time-lag and long runs associated with roller printing. This was quite evident in the 'I'm backing Britain Campaign' of 1968 when fabrics, banners, badges, etc., were designed and produced within a week or two of the first announcements.

The development of the teenage market was shown by such symptoms as Teenage Textiles, Furnishing Boutiques, Boudoir-tiques, Sub-Teen Textiles, Fabrics for Chubbies, Adolescent Adjuncts and many other long- and short-lived trends.

The upsurge of boutiques, at first as shoe-string shops, but later sponsored by finance groups or under the umbrellas of the larger stores, encouraged the rapid change of patterns and styles. Four distinct classes of textiles emerged. The first was for the wayout client, the avant-garde and customers with money, all of whom required the latest in trends and were prepared to replace very quickly with the next trend.

The second was for the boutique market supposedly catering for the teenage in years or spirit. This market offered great opportunity to the enterprising and gifted designer. Much of the designing for this market has been, and is, the most original produced. Often ingenious in treatment and colouring, it has been difficult for the designers to move away from contemporary Art Nouveau. As, however, each year new customers arrive, this factor may not matter for some time. There are signs that the sophistication of this type of designing is now being extended to the sub-teenage market, which may, of course, herald a complete change of inspiration.

The third is the type of textile design most successfully introduced by the Young Liberty Fabrics and the Young Sanderson Fabric Collection. These retain the clear colour quality and the main design aspects of each trend, but preserve the more conventional utilitarian qualities of a practical textile for use in the home. Pat Albeck designed for Sandersons in 1969 and an innovation was a textile with a number of border patterns based in peasant designs, giving an infinite variation on a 'Make Your Own Border' theme. The majority of these textiles were screen printed (see plate 82).

The fourth class was that once known as the backbone of the textile trade, the steady, bread and butter lines of popular printed textiles of all kinds. Some were reprints of designs first popular before 1900, others were rehashes of earlier designs brought up to date with respectable versions of the current vogue colours; others were safe designs upon floral and traditional themes, and still others were the various pictorial designs regularly produced for events, tourists and the souvenir trade. These range from handkerchiefs, scarves, tea cosies, oven gloves, bedspreads, glass and tablecloths to wall hangings and room dividers.

In addition to these popular textiles, the class also includes a great deal of the work of gifted but more orthodox designers who endeavoured to keep within the van of contemporary developments without departing too much from traditional acceptance.

Two societies, the Royal Society of Arts and the Council of Industrial Design, have done much to rouse intelligent interest and so to raise the general level of design standards and particularly in printed and woven textiles.

In screen printing mechanization has so far outstripped the financial capability of firms to re-equip that improved inventions are often waiting to be adopted. Germany and Switzerland in particular made large advances in automatic screen printing. The long tables with screens following each other down the full-piece length of forty or more yards were so much more economic for shorter runs than the older 'surface' machines employing wooden rollers with the design raised in felt and outlined in copper that they were universally adopted for such work (see plate 89).

It was not long before the screens stayed still and the fabric moved underneath. By this method some 160 yds of cloth could be printed, in up to ten colours, per hour and the table reduced to some 4 or 5 yds in length.

This was followed by an Austrian vertical, duplex, screen printing machine where twin, exactly registering, screens clamped to each side of the cloth and enabled one to print very wide and thick materials such as quilts, blankets or carpets on both sides at once. It has been used most successfully with pigment colours.

The need to obtain increased production speeds, without the sacrifice of the other advantages that screen printing presented, resulted in the introduction of forms of roller screen printing, but early machines had certain limitations, not least in the construction of the screens themselves.

About five years ago the Stork Company of Holland, one of Europe's biggest textile-machinery manufacturers, pioneered a new form of rotary screen printer which represents a major breakthrough in this field. This process involves the printing of colour through a constantly rotating cylindrical screen, thus replacing the intermittent motion of the mechanical flat screen machines. These cylindrical metal screens are mounted horizontally along the machine and when printing revolve in contact with an endless belt underneath, which carries the cloth into and through a drying chamber. The colours are pumped into each screen under automatic level control at a rate varying according to the requirement of the design (see plate 90).

Flat screen printing machines produce at about 350 yds per hour and up to twenty-one different colours, whereas the rotary screen machines print at speeds up to 2400 yds per hour and up to twenty different colours. The older roller printer could print 1200 yds per hour and up to eighteen different colours.

The first of these Stork machines was installed in the Sanderson works in March of 1967, and was followed by a second similar machine in March 1968.

D. G. Kale mentions other methods under development including photo printing, by projection or by contact (Photone process) and multi-colour surface printing with one roller or block.[1]

A limited market still exists for the actual hand-block print which is literally a fabric printed by hand. It is a slow and meticulous process, the design being traced on to a series of wooden blocks, each colour having a separate block. Again, a large block can be divided for ease of handling by the printer.

A block is made up of layers of wood, the top layer, the one the blockmaker works on, is sycamore, because it must be fine grained and must not split or chip. It also has to stand up to hammering while printing, and continual 'washing' after printing.

Blocks have 'pitch pins' to ensure that each is located correctly when printing, but with even the best craftsman there are slight variations which give the

[1] Kale D. G. *Principles of Cotton Printing* Bombay, 1957, pp 94–103

fabrics a 'living' quality and a third dimension which helps to distinguish a hand-block print.

In 1968 the Courtauld Educational Trust sponsored a research project on unconventional fabrics proposed by Professor Roger Nicholson of the School of Textile Design and its Textile and Fashion Research Unit of the Royal College of Art. The results of this research were shown in an exhibition of Design Development for the Textile Industry held at the R.C.A. Galleries, Kensington Grove, London, in November 1968. In his introduction to the catalogue Professor Nicholson gave a clear picture of the possible developments in textiles over the next decade. '. . . The last decade has produced major changes within the textile industry. Perhaps the most significant development has been the formation of larger textile groups. This has resulted in increased research and development and produced great technical advance—a progress still gathering momentum.

'In colleges design always has the greatest priority but more than ever before it must also originate through the new techniques of manufacture; as new processes emerge from research it is essential that the designer and technologist can operate as a team capable of evolving original yet practical ideas . . .

'In the next decade one can expect even greater changes, and in particular the use of computers to aid the design process. When this occurs, it is easy to imagine some of the outcome in terms of: problem definition; physical and functional solutions; control of a synthesis of techniques including many which are at the moment thought of as being outside the normal scope of the textile industry; and the development of entirely new materials and methods of manipulating them into products . . .

'The training of the designer at present at College must be related to this industrial expansion over the next decade. He will have the choice of a career on a grand industrial scale or in pioneering his own more élite productions. In some of the work shown in the exhibition, student designers have worked in collaboration with other universities and textile firms and with Courtaulds development units. Not all these ventures have yet been taken far enough, but they have all been valuable educationally and help to set a precedent for training and research.

'The Textile and Fashion Research Unit is now well established within the College and its work should do a great deal to fuse together the different elements of the total textile design problem. It could extend more widely some of the design and technical innovations suggested by the work of this exhibition. It could integrate the work of the present-day designer with the techniques and possibilities of the future.'[1]

In the exhibition, apart from displays of more conventional textiles designed by past and present students, were the experimental results of collaboration between student designers and industry. These included: 1. Chromatographic

[1] Nicholson *An Exhibition of Design Development for the Textile Industry* RCA, 1968

Printing, which exploited the relationship between dye and fibre properties and fabric construction to give a widely different range of effects. 2. Appliqué fabrics combining orthodox printing methods with resin bonding and the subsequent application of metallized materials. 3. Devore, a process which removes partially or completely the printed area of fabric. The basic fabric is constructed with two chemically different yarns, one of which is resistant to the printed chemical. Effects are possible which cannot be achieved in any other way. 4. Glass Fibre fabrics which are widely used as drapes, as they have excellent flame resistance. This experiment involved the two types of yarn available by employing two-colour pad-dyeing to exploit the different pigment take-up of the textured and untextured yarns. 5. Paper fabrics having a great commercial potential which has not yet been sufficiently exploited. The relatively high production costs for a throw-away article and the problem of handling qualities seem to have prevented the acceptance of the fabric for everyday use in Europe. 6. Bonded Fibre wall coverings to provide thermal and sound insulation as well as a decorative surface. 7. Non-woven floor tiles of 100 per cent Courtelle needle-punched felt, printed with designs, impregnated with resin and produced as a floor covering in tile form. The designs were based on rotational repeats producing random patterns within the system. 8. Unconventional Systems of making high-cost exclusive fabrics produced by hand or simple mechanical systems. The aim of the proto-types was contrary to the objective of mass production. They employed known techniques and yet could also use recent technical developments such as lamina-tion, stitching, welding and die cutting. It was obvious that some present-day designers working in these methods would need to establish their own produc-tion units. 9. Permutational Printing, an attempt to use the cross-multiplication of design forms to provide an increased variety of pattern without an increase of production costs. Wide variations are possible on limited themes that use only a few screens in automatic screen printing systems. 10. Cross Printing, which exploits fabrics constructed with yarns having different dye take-up which can be cross-dyed and cross-printed to give design and colour variations with the advantage of longer production runs. 11. Spraying Techniques, first used after the Great War when a spray gun was used to spray the colour through a stencil design on to the fabric with the use of compressed air. This gave attractive shaded effects, especially if combined with controlled 'edge stencilling' or 'stip-pling'. Further development could incorporate stencil screens with mechanized controls or electronically controlled spray lines. The stencils could be on the fabric or as a tramway to control the spray jets under electronic control. Automatic colour change and shading would also be a possibility. 12. Non-woven or bonded fabric design development, which is possible in a number of ways including the use of die-cut patterns, design permutations using a limited number of printing screens and three-dimensional folding and lamination. 13. Die-cut Fabric constructions illustrating the manipulation of sheet plastic into a highly decorative textile by using a single die-cut motif interlaced by hand to produce a strong, flexible textile for use as a fashion or furnishing fabric. 14.

Arachne stitch bonded fabrics employing a basic web on to which the pattern is stitched in layers of areas of coloured fibre and other materials to give a considerable variety of weights and textures. 15. Translucent fabrics showing the possibility of using new plastic filament yarns in weaving. Subsequent printing and textural treatment could give partial see-through textiles.

Heal's, Liberty's and Sanderson's

The development of textile printing has depended upon the experience and influence of a large number of individual firms. The following accounts are not intended to be comprehensive but merely to illustrate the contribution of a number of these to the general evolution of the craft in Great Britain. A number of published books already deal with such noted firms as Stead, McAlpin and Company Ltd and other pioneers.

HEAL'S
A firm which has had a marked influence upon textile design as well as upon all forms of craftwork and particularly furniture is Heal's. It has steadily grown from the modest feather-dressing firm established by John Harris Heal in 1810 which moved in 1840 to a property, miller's stables and an old farmhouse, standing in a pleasant flower and fruit garden in Tottenham Court Road, London, to the present large store completed in 1962 upon the original site.

Sir Ambrose Heal (1872–1959) was a man of vision who changed the firm's approach to furniture design. He had served an apprenticeship at Warwick as a cabinet-maker and joined the family firm in 1893. His first pieces of simple oak furniture, dubbed by the salesmen as 'prison furniture', were a major success at the Art and Crafts Society's exhibitions. With Sir Gordon Russell he has had an undoubted influence on the fundamentals of functional design. In 1941 the firm concentrated on the production of printed furnishing fabrics and quickly gained a reputation for their printed designs, many of which won awards at international exhibitions. They have been particularly successful at anticipating trends in design and colour (see plates 51 and 70).

LIBERTY & CO LTD
This noted firm, always at the forefront in textile designing, traces its family history back to a young Corsican in 1400. The actual founder, Arthur Lazenby Liberty, was employed at a shop in Regent Street in 1862, and went to the second Great International Exhibition in South Kensington where the Victoria and Albert Museum now stands. He was particularly attracted to the Japanese art section and became manager of the Oriental Workshop opened by his employers next door to their Regent Street shop. Oriental art was the vogue in Paris and

had been brought to London by the American artist M. Whistler (1834–1903), who had settled there in 1859. Others, such as the Rossettis, caught the craze and became leaders in a new and long-lived study of Japanese prints, drawings, lacquer, porcelain, bronzes, silk, fans and bric-à-brac.

In 1875 Liberty opened his own shop, also in Regent Street, and by the end of the century this had become the best-known establishment for its avant-garde attitude to design. Once he was established he added to his Oriental stock other items such as rugs from the Middle East, embroidery and lace from Greece and Malta, and then, as he became more and more involved with the Aesthetic Movement as it came to be called, his success was assured. William Morris, the Rossettis, Whistler, Watts, Burne-Jones, Leighton, Alma Tadema and other leading artists of the day were regular callers at the shop as well as Carlyle, Ruskin, du Maurier and the architect Norman Shaw. His stock reflected the East and, when he found, in 1882, that the delicacy of the colouring of the imported cloths was becoming lost as a result of what was thought to be the European demand for cruder colours, he began to conduct experiments in dyeing Indian silks and cashmeres in this country as well as the difficult task of persuading British manufacturers to reproduce both ancient and original designs in materials corresponding to his own suggestions. Sometimes he had to supervise every stage in the process and almost stand over the workmen to see that they reproduced the goods he wanted. He revived some of the ancient dyeing techniques, notably those of Persia, and the weaving processes of the East were modified and adapted to the machine-woven fabrics of the English midlands. He chose first-class designers for his textiles, including Godwin, Voysey, Lindsay Butterfield, Sidney Mawson, Arthur Wilcock, Arthur Silver, Harry Napper and Alan Vigers, and became known in Europe and particularly in Paris with the Art Nouveau style (*Le Style Liberté*) and Italy (*Stile Liberty*). In 1889 he opened a branch in Avenue de L'Opera, Paris, to commemorate the Paris Exhibition, which lasted until 1931 (see plates 57 and 58).

Dissatisfied with controlling the work of many manufacturers to his own high standards, he eventually founded his own print works, near to those of Morris, at Merton Abbey, where he could completely supervise the production of the silks and furnishing fabrics for which his shop had become internationally famous. Wood-block prints of headsquares and the development of the Paisley pattern were particular favourites.

Liberty died in 1917, but the firm has been continued under other members of the family and developed its interest in contemporary styles with exhibitions of work by the Royal College of Art; by the famous Italian architect and designer, Gio Ponti; by Scandinavian designers; by Venetian glass-makers and West German craftsmen.

They have also developed a series of textiles designs called Young Liberty, specifically aimed at the present-day fashion. The print works at Merton have been substantially modernized and are now fully equipped for the printing of textiles by both hand-screen and automatic screen printing methods.

ARTHUR SANDERSON & SONS LTD

Sanderson's are an exceptional firm not only in the wallpapers and textiles they produce but in the excellent manner in which both their own products and textiles from other manufacturers in the United Kingdom, Europe and North America are displayed in their well-designed London showrooms in Berners Street. They are also outstanding in the co-operation they have always extended to textile students both at Berners Street and in organized visits to their wallpaper factory at Perivale and their furnishing fabrics print works at Uxbridge.

The firm commenced in 1860 when Arthur Sanderson imported and traded in high-class French wallpapers from Soho Square, London. In 1865 the firm moved to Berners Street and opened a wallpaper factory at Chiswick, which was in operation until it was destroyed by fire in 1928. Rebuilt in 1930 at Perivale, it has been steadily enlarged over the years and produces both hand-block, screen-printed and roller-printed papers of all types.

In 1921 the Uxbridge works commenced production by specializing in roller prints by a new printing process hitherto not used for calico printing. In 1934 weaving was added, to be followed by Jacquard weaving in 1950.

As well as roller printing there is a fully automatic screen printing process in operation and recently Sandersons have installed a number of the latest Stork rotary screen printers supplied by the Stork Company of Scotland. These are capable of printing up to 2400 yds per hour as against the 350 yds per hour of flat screen printing.

An interesting development in design has been the reissue by Sanderson's in slightly adapted widths and colours of original designs by eminent nineteenth-century designers such as Lewis F. Day (Strongstry, Holcombe, Greenmount and Helmshore, first produced by him during 1895–1904, and based on the curving lines of the art nouveau movement of the time); Allan F. Viger (Pansy and Shrewsbury), and William Morris (Chrysanthemum, Batchelors' Button and Marigold) (see plates 79 and 80).

DEVELOPMENTS ABROAD

Although the general pattern of textile printing was followed in most European countries, certain individual characteristics caused divergencies in practice, which were even more strangely marked in other continents. The following accounts supplement the history already given.[1]

Eire

An interesting experiment was commenced in Ireland in 1961 when the Irish Export Board invited five Scandinavian designers and design teachers to Kilkenny. From this arose the Kilkenny Design Workshops established in 1965 with the aims of raising the standards of the country's industrial design in the crafts. A magnificent eighteenth-century stables has been converted into an impressive design centre with five workshops engaged in design and its practical application to weaving, silversmithing, ceramics, wood-turning and textile printing. To this centre come visitors to buy conventional art handicraft goods, but the chief purpose of the workshops is to improve the design of Irish industrial products, not by the imposition of Scandinavian designs but by the provision of designs for industry and the training of young designers in graphic and craft design.

France

We have no records or specimens of French printed textiles dating from much before the middle of the seventeenth century. Unsubstantiated references exist in plenty, but inventions of earlier periods give the word *imprimé* in relation to hangings and it is by no means certain if this refers to printed as distinct from stamped or pressed textiles.[2] P. R. Schwartz and R. de Micheauiex in their book *A Century of French Fabrics 1850–1950* state that in France 'the term *indiennes* (chintz) is found in Marseilles inventories since at least 1580, and on 22 June 1648, a card-maker and engraver of this town was associated with the "dyeing of cloth to make *indiennes*". Thus it is quite possible that southern France is, in fact, the birth-place of European calico-printing.' This is a quite possible hypothesis, as it is known that a number of Armenian printers from the Levant, men who were familiar with mordant printing on vegetable fibres and direct printing on animal fibres, were established in Marseilles at this time.

As has already been mentioned, the visits of the Siamese envoys to Versailles

---

[1] Such information is most difficult to find for the smaller countries or those no longer in existence. The author would welcome further sources to supplement this section
[2] *CIBA Review* 31, pp 1090 ff

in the 1680s accentuated the interest in the Indian and Levantine cloths of painted gold with brilliant colours and intricate designs. Cargoes of these calicoes and silks had been brought back since the 1630s by Portuguese merchants who had undertaken the long and dangerous sea voyages to the East and back.

The genuine and costly Oriental fabrics were coveted by the nobility, but the common people had to be content with the copies of the originals which were extensively produced by French manufacturers. The practice of block printing had been well established on the Continent and official records in Rouen mention printed linens and cottons as early as 1688, when lawsuits were brought against local craftsmen for contravening the laws against calico printing passed in 1686. These were not finally removed until 1759.

These laws referred only to cotton and it was not until printers switched their printing to linen and other cloths that further decrees were issued up to 1708, when a final decree was published forbidding the total manufacture, import, trade in and use of every kind of *toiles peintes* in France. In the State Archives of Paris are reports of persons who were heavily fined for contravening these laws: one, a clerk, was fined 200 livres for wearing a red-flowered dressing-gown, and another, a lady's maid, the same sum for wearing a printed dress.

M. Juvet-Michel puts forward an interesting hypothesis to explain the action of the French Government.[1] Whereas the banning of imports was sensible in that it conserved currency, the prohibition of manufacture would appear to ruin a young and rising industry, close factories, and cause unemployment and the destroying of hundreds of printing blocks. The French Government therefore, must have had other, hidden, reasons and he suggests that it was most important to ensure that only products of the very best quality were manufactured and sold abroad at the highest profit possible. The new industry sold at a price little higher than unprinted material and its products were inferior to, and a poor imitation of, foreign goods. The silk and wool trades, however, produced good profits from reliable products and, since the repeal of the Edict of Nantes, had lost a large number of skilled workers and could ill afford to lose others.

There were certain areas of France that received permission to continue by virtue of old regulations applying to the *enclos privilégiés*. These were areas surrounding churches and monasteries which were enclosed with walls and gates. The police could not enter these areas without permission. The manufacturers and traders in the forbidden fabrics established themselves in these areas and this, together with bribery to the officials of the courts who bought the cloths confiscated by the same courts and sold them to the highest bidder, ensured a regular supply of counterfeit cloths. In 1664 the *Compagnie des Indes Orientales* had been founded by Jean-Baptiste Colbert (1619–83), the Comptroller-General under King Louis XIV. This company was permitted to import and sell genuine Oriental fabrics. In addition, large quantities were smuggled into the country from Holland, Switzerland, England and Germany—a dangerous occupation punishable by the galleys or death.

[1] *CIBA Review* 31, pp 1090 ff

In the Rouen area a dyehouse proprietor, one Jacques le Marcis, was granted a royal privilege in 1729 'to dye, print and furnish with flower patterns in any colours wool fabrics of French origin'.[1] These he printed from copper plates. In 1749 a *Manufacture du Nid-de-Chien* specializing in flowered fabrics was established in the same area and by 1767 had begun calico printing. Further factories operated illegally in the Bondeville valley in the 1760s using wood blocks and resist styles. The decrees were flouted and *indiennes* continued to grow in popularity, despite the heavier fines imposed, the ripping off by the police of the offending print dresses from the backs of women walking in the streets and the destroying of stocks of garments. This strange situation fluctuated over a period of years until 5 September 1759, when general permission was granted to print patterns on woven fabrics, subject for a time to industrial taxes and other restrictions.

As soon as the ban was lifted calico-printing establishments sprang up all over France and particularly in Alsace, Lyons, Nantes, Paris and Normandy. Many of the printed cloths produced at this time were patterned with dashes and dots or circles and ovals in reds, violets, yellows, blues, black, gold, and silver. Apart from certain blue-reds, the black and the metals, most of these colours and their mixtures have faded badly in surviving samples.

In order to improve the imitation *indiennes* it was necessary to experiment and in France experimentation had been severely curtailed by the excessive restrictions upon home printing. In certain other countries in Europe no such harsh laws had been passed and so it was to expert foreign specialists from Germany, Holland, and particularly Switzerland, that France turned for help in undertaking such work as pattern designing, copper engraving and finishing, and the training of her own printers. A beginning in the training of apprentices was frustrated partly by the reluctance of the foreign craftsmen to teach their skills and by the events before, during and after the Revolution. This caused most of the smaller print works to close down. The setting up of a new print works when comparative peace returned was often costly. Many of the new factories planned so as to operate on a mass-production basis were formed by companies rather than individuals. The Republic encouraged such enterprise and new factories mushroomed all over the country for a few years. They printed linen and cloth with emblems of the Revolution. Technical knowledge was supplied by the descendants of the French *émigrés* who had fled to Switzerland after the repeal of the Edict of Nantes in 1685. These men, together with other skilled Swiss technicians, left Switzerland to work in French factories, bringing with them all the knowledge developed in a country that had not been hindered and frustrated by more than seventy years of restrictions.

The first important factory established before the Revolution was founded by Johann Rudolph Wetter in 1744 just outside Marseilles, followed by another in 1758 at Orange. This factory produced the cloths that became famous as *toiles d'Orange*. Wetter is recorded as a man of wide artistic interests who employed

[1] *CIBA Review* 135, p 27

artists and maintained a salon with concerts and performances of contemporary and classical music and drama.

Another noted printer was Abraham Frey at Rouen and Troyes in 1758. The Petitpierre brothers opened a factory at Nantes about the same time.

The most famous cloth printer and dyer in eighteenth-century France was Christophe Phillippe Oberkampf (1738–1815), who came from Switzerland. As a young man he had worked in a variety of famous dyehouses and eventually in 1760 had founded his own dyehouse and factory in an old house at Jouy en Josas on the river Bière near Versailles. He realized that to succeed as a cloth printer he must produce goods of quality both in design and fastness. He travelled extensively, assiduously culling ideas from all over Europe until he had researched into all the available types of machinery and all the known dye chemistry of the time. He built up the finest-equipped and best-run works in France, with social welfare for his employees, in what was eventually to become a small town producing the famed *toiles de Jouy*.

At first these had been called *toiles d'Orange de Jouy*, partly to catch the fame of the products of Wetters' factory at Orange and partly in imitation of the imported cloths known as Siamese or *Siamoises*. It was not long, however, before the fabrics could stand on their own repute. Oberkampf exported to and visited England, Holland, Belgium, Scandinavia, Spain, Germany and other countries.

After the fall of Napoleon and the death of Oberkampf in 1815, the factory came under the control of Oberkampf's son and the firm's chemist Samuel Widmer, who had discovered the so-called 'solid green' to replace the combination of blue and green previously used. But economic conditions had worsened during the last years of the war against England, money had become scarce, workmen had been drafted into the army, the factory plundered by the allies, and the new directors were unable to keep pace with the rapid development of textile printing in Alsace and Normandy. It eventually closed down in 1843.

The designs used in the *toiles de Jouy* were many and varied. They present a most revealing panorama of the various aesthetic trends in Europe over a continuous period of more than half a century. Since many of them were repeated again and again until the end of the nineteenth century by other printers, and since Oberkampf had often reissued earlier designs with slight modifications usually in the popular colours of a period, it is possible to see the total development of design, colour and techniques for a considerable period in both exclusive and mass-produced textiles (see plate 28).

Once the ban upon chintzes was lifted in 1759, designers began to introduce designs at first based upon the exotic imported Oriental patterns and later including what became typically French motifs such as fluttering ribbons, baskets, garlands, delicately entwined vignettes, twisting flowers and native birds, as well as sprig patterns from flowers, leaves, herbs and grasses.

Wood blocks were able to give only clumsy imitations of both the hand-painted Eastern textiles and the light and airy woven patterns of the French workers in silk. With the introduction of soft copper plates and then copper cylinders it was possible to engrave much more finely. The earlier stiff and rather formal designs gradually became much more relaxed and flowing.

The rococo quality of the early sprig patterns continued in popularity throughout the whole of the period from the 1790s to the late 1850s. At a slightly later date a baroque manner with large garlands of flowers gradually came into use as the size of the copper plates increased.

The most uniformly popular style of chintz was undoubtedly the stripe pattern with flowers, flowing ribbons and small motifs between the stripes. These were sometimes wide, at other times narrow, sometimes horizontal, sometimes vertical. Stripes were especially popular and particularly so at the time of Marie Antoinette, when many variations of the negligée type of robe and dress, called the *Polonaise* or *à la Turque* styles used these designs. Louis XVI (1754–93) was so enamoured of the *toiles de Jouy* that the ladies-in-waiting wore court dresses made of the lightest printed fabrics and the gentlemen wore print dressing-gowns, coats, waistcoats and other garments to such an extent that a contemporary book reported in 1788 that all those present at court were like zebras.

Madame de Pompadour (1721–64), the patron of the *Compagnie des Indes*, encouraged the vogue for the block-printed chinoiserie patterns with strange mythical creatures and exotic plants, bringing an Oriental style to furniture and wall coverings. By the late 1770s this had given way to an interest in rustic motifs of landscapes with mills, pastoral scenes and similar subjects. The smaller patterns in particular exploited a new technique called *picotage*. This filled in the spaces between the pattern units with a background of brass pins which, driven into the block, printed as tiny dots. Sometimes designs were entirely carried out in such dots; in others the background was left white and bouquets of flowers were printed at some little distance from each other.

Later still in the 1780s the fashion moved to allegorical scenes and in the 1790s these were followed by such contemporary subjects as the fall of the Bastille in 1789, the American War of Independence and the ascent of the Montgolfière Balloon in 1783. These *camieux*, as they were known when printed in the popular style of one colour only, usually red, black or porcelain blue on white, are seen at their best in the work of Jean Baptiste Huet (1745–1811). From 1783 he was the principal designer at Oberkampf's works where he introduced many new and original motifs. By employing fine drawing, easy flowing links between individual scenes together with the ability to capture upon the copper plate the sparkle of the original red chalk drawings, he set new and high standards of design. His particularly individual style was copied by every other factory in France and abroad. The term *toile de Jouy* was universally applied to this type of printed fabric wherever and by whom it was produced.

One of his most interesting designs was one in the single-colour red, giving a view of the process in use at the Jouy factory. Various pictures show lengths of unprinted calico pegged out on the grass during bleaching, a small factory by the river so essential for a constant supply of good water, workmen damping and beating cloth, block printing, and other views (see plate 23).

1

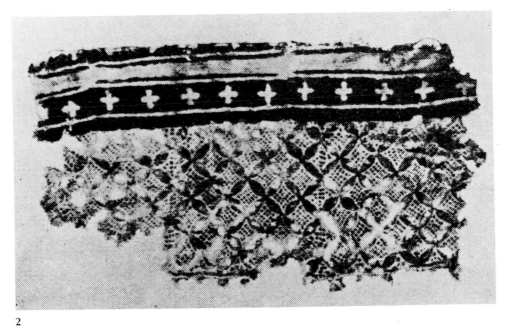

2

1   Child's tunic of printed cloth. Achmim. 4th century AD.

2   Border and centre pattern of the oldest known two-colour print, in red and black. From the burial grounds of Achmim (Panapolis) in Upper Egypt. 6th or 7th century AD.

3

4

3 Wooden printing block from Achmim. The two ends of the cylindrical block bear the patterns. 4th century AD.

4 Printing block found in the grave of a textile printer showing stylized peacocks with Tree of Life. Achmim. 7th or 8th century AD.

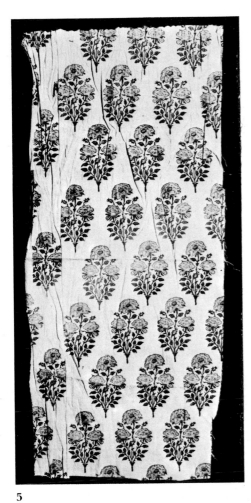

5

6

5 Fragment of a dress fabric, possibly part of a
   jāma (man's robe) Block printed on a
   ground impressed with a diamond trellis.
   North India, Delhi. Early 18th century.

6 A typical Tree of Life design on a fine
   cotton bedcover outlined with a stencil and
   painted in colour by hand. On the back is the
   stamp of the Honourable (United) East
   India Company factory at Masulipatam,
   Madras Presidency. 144″ x 92″. 1750 AD.

7 A *kalka* design from Kum ba konam,
   Madras. Wood-block print of floral design.
   19th century.

7

8

8 Painted cotton bedspread or *palampore*. Made in India for the Western
market *c*. 1620 AD.

9

10

9 Armenian cotton dorsal cloth for an altar. Pattern, showing the biblical story of man, produced by a combination of indigo dyeing (on a resist applied, in part at least, by means of blocks) and mordant dyeing. In red, yellow, brown, blue and white on a blue ground. 60″ x 114″. Uncertain date: 1310 AD or possibly early 17th or 18th century.

10 The Tapestry of Sion. Section of dancers and horsemen of a mural hanging, probably from the episcopal palace of Sion. North Italian print on linen. 14th century.

11

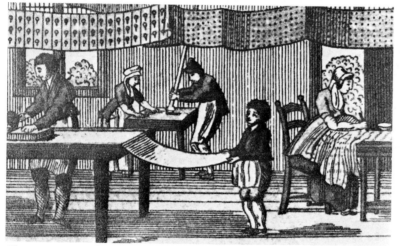

12

13

14

Jacob Stampe liuing at ij Sighn of the Callico
Printer in Hounsditch Prints all sorts of
Callicoes Lineings Silkes Stuffs
New or Ould at Reasonable Rates

11 A wood-block print probably depicting bird-snaring scenes; possibly Flemish. Late 14th-early 15th century.

12 Printing, painting and lustring chintz. It was in these print-shops that the so-called chintz papers were made as a sideline to cloth printing. The technique was much the same, but the pieces were smaller; the machines which permit the manufacture of paper of any length had not yet been invented. From a woodcut of 1750.

13 A workman scraping the flour and starch off the fabric after dyeing. From an engraving in Roland de la Platière's *L'Art de préparer et d'imprimer les Etoffes de laine*, 1780.

14 The trade card of Jacob Stampe. Late 17th century.

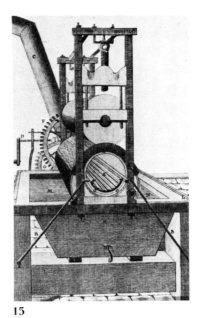

15   16

17   18

15   A French machine for printing on wool fabrics, invented by J.-A. Bonvallet of Amiens *c.* 1780. From an engraving in the *Encyclopédie méthodique*, Paris, 1782.

16   The so-called *Bois Protat*, a French printing block. 9″ x 24″. Late 14th century. Discovered in 1900 in Sennecy.

17   A *dymki* print from Modrý Kameň, Ruthenia. Black oil print from wood blocks on rough unbleached linen. Mid 19th century.

18   Counterpane of printed calico by John Hewson. American, late 18th century.

19   Block print in vegetable colours on rough linen; called a *noboyka* print. 17th century.

19

20

21

22

23

20 Handkerchief plate printed with 'Stage of Europe December 1812'. English.

21 Handkerchief plate printed with 'The Eastern Question 1878'. When folded into four (22) the answer to the question 'who will solve it?' appears: Disraeli. English.

23 J. B. Huet's famous design *Les travaux de la manufacture, Oberkampf* made in 1785 for the Oberkampf factory at Jouy. It shows scenes from the factory. Top row from left to right: preparing the cotton; engraved copper plate printing; the factory and village of Jouy with cloth lying out to bleach. Second row: dye and fixing vats; smoothing and rolling; designing; touching-in colours; rinsing. Third row: Oberkampf's offices; lessons for children of the workmen; the drying house; steeping and collecting up. Bottom row: part of the factory building; bleaching and pounding the cotton; block printing by hand; a press; mixing dyes.

24

25

26

24 One of the five surviving English textiles which can be dated from the inscriptions incorporated in the design. Printed from copper plates by Robert Jones in 1769 with colours added by wood-blocks and pencilling. Inscribed 'R. IONES & Co. Iany 1st 1769' and 'R. IONES & Co. Old Ford'. 90″ x 36″.

25 *L'art d'Aimer*. Nantes, 1788. This plate-print was by Favre, Petitpierre et Cie.

26 *Fleurs indiennes*. Block print by A. Guesnel, Darnetal near Rouen 1765. Notice the *Bon Teint* stamp at the top.

27

27 Striped floral chintz typical of a style popular during the last decade of the 18th century. It is block-printed in madder colours on cotton with pencilled blue at Fordingbridge, Hants. 3 blue warp threads in each selvedge. *c.* 1790.

28   Block print on *Toile de Jouy. c.* 1775.

29   Wood-block print on cotton in the *chinoiserie* style. *c.* 1770.

30   Horace Vernet's design *La Chasse*, copper plate on cotton, in which he developed the effect of depth to imitate a painting. Jouy, 1815.

31

31 Blue plate-printed chintz of about 1805 adapted from Robert Smirke's *Seven Ages of Man* used by Boydell in his Shakespeare's Gallery 1801. Signed Slack (for John Slack, engraver, Salford).

32 Block print of 1775 produced with iron and alumina mordants in conjunction with subsequent madder dyeing. The yellow shades were produced by padding after prior resist printing of specific areas. The resisted medallions of the relief block-printed portion contain scenes from the fable of *The Fox and the Stork*.

32

33

33 Block-printed in the madder style on linen with pencilled blue and yellow showing the high standard that was achieved in the 1770s. Although the actual printer is not known it is close in style and drawing to a number of wood block impressions in a Crayford calico printer's pattern book *c.* 1775.

34 'Palm Tree and Pheasant'. Block-
   printed in madder colours on a 'tea-
   ground' at Bannister Hall. English,
   1815.

34

35

35 'Gothic Windows'. Roller-printed on
   glazed cotton in red, pink (stippled),
   ochre, brown, blue, purple, double
   green. Length of repeat 26″. English,
   1830.

36

37

38

Iohn Wildblood at the Rainbow &
3 pidgons in St Clements Lane
In Lombard Street London who
Married the Widdow Harrinton
Silk Dyer

39

Mary & Ann Hogarth
from the old Frock shop the corner of the
Long Walk facing the Cloysters, Removed
to ye Kings Arms joyning to ye Little Britain-
gate near Long Walk Sells ye best & most Fashi
onable Ready Made Frocks, sutes of Fustian,
Ticken & Holland, stript Dimmity & Flanel
Wastcoats, blue & canvas Frocks & bluecoat Boys Dra.
Likewise Fustians, Tickens, Hollands, white
stript Dimitys, white & stript Flanels in ye piece.
by Wholesale or Retale, at Reasonable Rates.

40

36 A striking example of the elaborate discharge prints which were popular about 1805 and which illustrate the fine work then possible with wood-block prints. It is a white discharge printed on an indigo ground and appears in a pattern-book containing many such prints in the possession of the Calico Printers' Association, Manchester.

37 Pattern of a chintz by Japuis and Son, France. Exhibited at the Great Exhibition of 1851. 'The specimen of French Chintz which we now engrave is a favourable example of the taste and propriety of design bestowed by our Continental neighbours upon articles, which, in our own country, have long been characterized by an absence of that essential quality. The draperies of printed and glazed cotton known by the name of chintz have, indeed, too often exhibited the most flagrant and glaring improprieties.' From the official *Descriptive and Illustrated Catalogue*, London, 1851.

38 Block printed discharge on a dark cotton ground. Logwood then printed on. English, *c.* 1805.

39 Trade card of John Wildblood, dyer of silk. Probably late 17th century.

40 Trade card of Mary and Ann Hogarth advertising their Frock Shop. Late 18th century.

41

41 This floral chintz, roller-printed in Lancashire in 1835, illustrates the fashion for large, precisely drawn flowers, which is also found in English wood-block prints from 1828-36.

42 'Strawberry Thief', William Morris's best known chintz design dating from 1883. It was his first design to be block-printed by the indigo-discharge method after he had taken up the printing of his own designs at Merton Abbey, Surrey.

42

43 Lino block-printed head
square designed by
Margaret Holgate,
printed by Patricia
Robinson, 1955.

43

44 Roller-printed cretonne
designed by Albert
Griffiths for W. Foxton,
1922.

44

45

46

45 A roller-printed discharge on manganese-bronze ground; other colours added by
surface roller. The birds were copied directly from Audubon's *Birds of America*.
(Manganese-bronze was invented by John Mercer in 1823.) Printed in Lancashire in
1831.

46 'Cherwell' a printed velveteen designed by William Morris, for Morris and Co. *c.* 1885.
It appears in their catalogue for 1909.

47

48   49

47   Printed velveteen, designed by Lewis F. Day, 1888, for Wardle's Art Prints 26″/27″ wide.

48   'Birds and strawberries' by C. F. A. Voysey c. 1895. Roller-printed (duplex print) in monochrome for Newman, Smith and Newman.

49   'Large blue flowers and leaves' by Lindsay P. Butterfield c. 1900. Roller-printed in colours by G. P. and J. Baker at the Swaisland Printing Works, Crayford.

50

51

52

53

50 Printed velveteen, designed by Alphonse Mucha (1860-1939) and printed by Messrs Hines, Stroud and Co. of Friday Street, London. 1899-1900.

51 'Extension', designed by Haydon Williams and screen-printed on shrink resistant cotton by Heal Fabrics Ltd, London, 1968. The design is based on a development of the sea shell and won a Design Centre Award.

52 'Bye, Bye Blackbird', screen printed on polished cotton and designed in the Sanderson Studios, is an attempt to re-create the era of the Hollywood Spectacular. Within the design are Technicolour birds, a musical back-cloth waterfall, cloud formations over rising or setting suns, exotic flowers and foliage. English, 1969.

53 Spray-printed design by Susan Saunders on a 'paper' blind. R. C. A./Courtaulds experimental work.

54

55

56

57

58

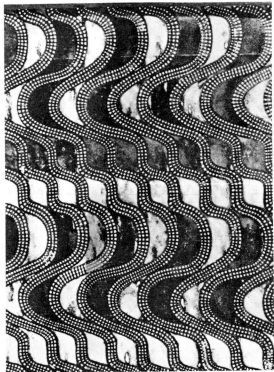

59

54 'Swirls in green and red' by Christopher Dresser, 1899. Roller-printed in colours by F. Steiner and Co.

55 'Purple and blue flowers on a blue background' by Harry Napper, c. 1900. Block-printed in colours by G. P. and J. Baker at the Swaisland Printing Works, Crayford.

56 'Cromer Bird' by A. H. Mackmurdo, c. 1884. Block-printed in colours by Simpson and Godlee, Manchester, for the Century Guild.

57 Printed cotton by Arthur Silver for Liberty & Co., c. 1896.

58 Roller-printed cotton by Arthur Wilcock for Liberty and Co., c. 1890. Printed by E. J. Buckley, Manchester, and used by Walter Crane in his dining room.

59 'Wave Pattern': a fabric design in pencil and water colour by Charles Rennie Mackintosh, 1917-1921.

60

61

62

63

60　'White': linen printed in colours. Designed by Vanessa Bell for the Omega Workshops and
　　printed in France, 1913.

61　'Magnolia blossom and butterflies.' a roller-printed cretonne designed by Sidney Haward
　　for Turnbull and Stockdale Ltd, 1920.

62　Cotton, roller-printed in colours. Designed by Minnie McLeish for W. Foxton Ltd, 1929.

63　Cotton, screen-printed in colours. Designed by Duncan Grant for Allan Walton Textiles,
　　1932.

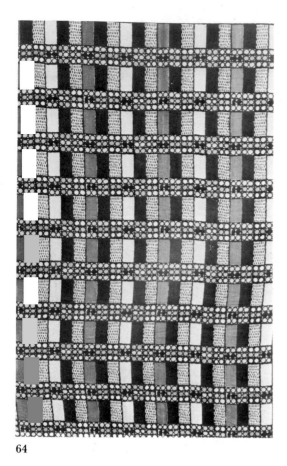

64

65

66

67

68

64 Cotton voile, roller-printed in red, yellow, green, brown and black on white. English, 1926. William Foxton.

65 Cotton, roller-printed in black on white ground. English, 1928. William Foxton.

66 'Pointed Pips.' Hand block-printed on linen. Designed and printed by Phyllis Barron and Dorothy Larcher. English, 1938.

67 Rayon or cotton, printed textile. David Whitehead Fabrics, 1953.

68 'Torrs', cotton, screen-printed. Designed for Edinburgh Weavers by Michael O'Connell, c. 1938.

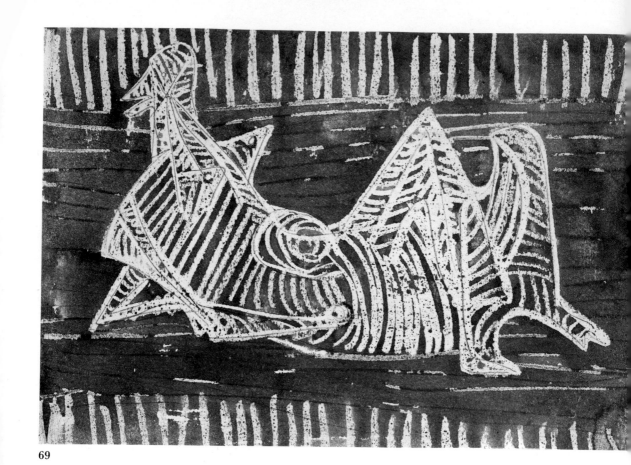

69

69 'Reclining figure': wall hanging designed by Henry Moore in 1944 for Ascher (London)
   Ltd.

70 'Lacy', 'Calyx' and 'Natura', three textiles from Heal & Son Ltd, London, c. 1950. 'Calyx',
   screen-printed in colours on linen was designed by Lucienne Day and received the
   International Award of the Museum of Modern Art, New York, for the best design of
   1951.

71 'Sunflower', screen-printed fabric designed by Howard Carter for Heal and Son Ltd, 1961.
   Winner of a Design Centre Award.

72 'Volta,' an African design by E. Ablade Glover screen-printed on cotton satin for
   Edinburgh Weavers, 1962.

70

71

72

73

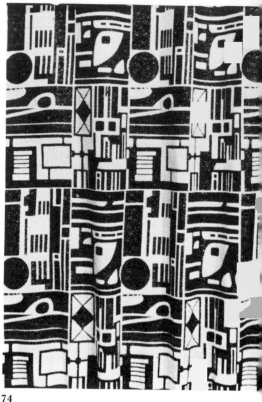

74

75

76

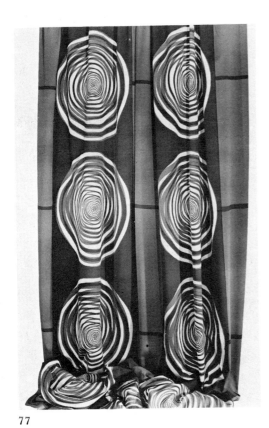

77

78

73 'Bianca,' a hand-print inspired by Texan cowboys and produced by Conran Fabrics, 1963.

74 Screen-print on acetate by Shunzo Tokuda, Terkoku Rayon Co., Japan, 1962.

75 'Op' design screen-printed in black and white on crêpe by Veronica Marsh, 1966.

76 'Shimmy,' designed by Natalie Gibson and screen-printed on cotton by Conran Fabrics Ltd.

77 'Centrum' designed by Molly White and screen-printed by Hull Traders Ltd., 1966.

78 'Paramount', produced in 1968 by Sanderson Fabrics reflected the interest in *Bonnie and Clyde, Thoroughly Modern Millie, The Boy Friend* and other aspects of the revival of Art Deco at this time.

79

80

81

79,80 Two versions of a textile revived by Sanderson. 'The Mallow' appears very different according to the background colour.

81   Screen print on rayon/linen. Designed by Raili Konttinen for Porin Puuvilla Oy, Finland, 1967.

82 'Babylon' screen-print on heavy cotton by Pat Albeck for Sanderson Fabrics, 1969.

83 Long narrow dress in African cotton and screen
   printed with a large single motif on front and back in
   green, pale yellow and dark red. By Veronica Marsh,
   1967.

84 'Melanie', screen-print on cotton satin for Bernard
   Wardle, 1968.

85 'Mykeno', screen-print on cotton satin by Linje
   Heming for Saini Salonen, Sweden, 1967.

83

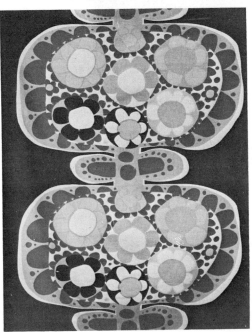

84

85

86

87

86 Japanese stencil of the late 18th century used somewhat in the manner of a silk-screen.

87 A block-printer at the Rosebank Works. Notice that the hammer is held upright.

88

88 A roller printer at the Uxbridge Works of Sandersons. Contemporary.

89

90

89 Flat screen printing at the Uxbridge Works of Sandersons. The fabric is gummed down to
the table and the screens automatically follow each other, printing along the fabric.
Numbered tubs containing dye stand behind the fabric and dye is poured from the tubs
into the screens as required. At the back can be seen cloth prepared for printing and the
rollers on which it was delivered. Contemporary.

90 Rotary screen printing with the new Stork machine at the Uxbridge Works of Sandersons.
The fabric passes under the cylindrical screens and the whole process is entirely automatic
with the printed fabric moving into the drying and fixation chambers at the top right of the
picture. Contemporary.

In 1791 the patterns became very striking, with large lozenges and zigzags completely at variance with previous taste. In 1793 there was a revival of Persian designs for export to England and in 1795 bronze grounds with a close pattern of plants and wild flowers became very popular. Another revival in 1806 was the technique of white resist printing on a blue ground used by Oberkampf's father in his own factory in Switzerland many years before. In 1809 there was the rather unhappy introduction of the solid green dye.

After the death of Huet the factory had great difficulty in replacing him and although the architect Hippolyte Lebas (1782–1867) produced a most popular print *Monuments de Paris* in 1816 and Horace Vernet (1789–1863) designed a hunting scene, *La Chasse*, in 1815, with a three-dimensional recession, the fabrics suffered a gradual decline from the death of the founder Oberkampf in 1815— when, as has already been described, the work of the factory was impaired by the effects of war—until the closure of the factory in 1843 (see plate 30).

Another noted but local printer of the period was J.-A. Bonvallet of Amiens who employed a press, similar to that used in book printing, to print wool and plush. Oberkampf introduced a similar machine into his factory at Jouy in 1780. Bonvallet was also one of the first to use a roller press, as described on page 25.

It is difficult to realize in these days of fast colours just how little knowledge was possessed by the early printers in France. The wooden blocks were often inadequate for other than relatively coarse designs and the dyes difficult to use from a block unless pigments were employed. These tended to give a heavy dull look and were often fugitive when washed. Even the new flat metal plates were often blurred at the edges, spoiling the repeats. Yet so insistent was the demand for fabrics *à la mode* that continual research went on into the techniques of printing, which culminated in the engraved and surface roller printing machines. With one of these machines, one man and one boy could turn out more than 5000 yds of cloth per day, working in a single large room. To hand print this amount in the same time would have required the full-time work of over forty copper-plate printers and a vast building.

Research was also necessary into the perfecting of the dyes. Customers naturally disliked fugitive colours and for a considerable time cloth-printing factories in France marked the borders of their fabrics either *bon teint* or *grands teints* to show a fast and durable colour and to distinguish them from the *petits teints* or *faux teints* where the colours, although often brighter and more attractive, were likely to fade and to wash badly. Strict regulations were enforced to maintain professional standards and the printers strove endlessly to discover more and more permanent dyes for printing. French workers do not appear to have followed the developments in Switzerland and England, using madder and other fast dyes with the appropriate mordants in the Oriental manner, until Oberkampf and Jouy. The prohibitions in force for so long most probably inhibited extensive experiments outside the exempted areas and, since these were small and overcrowded, inside as well (see plate 26).

Oberkampf often consulted the famous French chemist Claude Berthollet

(1748–1822) over both the bleaching properties of chlorine and his experiments in the art of dyeing. He also benefited from the many experiments, particularly in the use of Turkey red, conducted by Jean Antoine Claude Chaptal (1756–1832), founder of the first chemical factory in France and the first scientific organizer of technical research.

It is of interest that the substantial exports before and after the Revolution, although cheap and inferior, were used as trading goods with the colonies. The natives not only traded pearls, ivory and coral for pieces of print but the chiefs also traded their subjects as slaves. This was not officially ended until 1814.

After 1815 the calico-printing areas developed rapidly, particularly in the Rouen district, where the speciality was in fine cotton items, including scarves and handkerchiefs, using wood-block as well as the English roller machines or one of the many versions of the Perrotine. Colours were simple, including violet, red, puce and tobacco brown. Metal plates were later used for the production of pictorial handkerchiefs covering all possible types of subjects such as the Paris World Exhibition of 1889, the Eiffel Tower, mottoes, portraits, poems, maps, calendars, a Pocket Medical Instructor, Women's Rights and similar designs in much brighter colours.

The Perrotine was a printing machine that faithfully imitated the operations of a hand printer. It was invented in 1834 by a M. Perrot of Rouen, who was a mechanic and a calico printer. It printed from flat wooden blocks, but the pattern was not carved out of the wood but formed by metal coppering or the insertion into the block of metal strips and pins. It permitted the printing of many colours in one operation at a much greater speed and with much less wear and tear than was possible with all-wood blocks. Since the machine produced as much with three or five men working it as at least four dozen hand printers and assistants could produce in the same time, its use spread to many countries; it did not survive long, however, in competition with roller printing and only a few machines were left in operation after World War I. It had many advantages over hand-block printing and, in particular, avoided the inaccurate joining up of patterns and allowed the reprinting of faulty prints at once and exactly in registration (see diagram 7).

After Oberkampf and Jouy the printed textile industry in France had a similar history to that in England. The finely detailed pictures on cloth became mere illustrations that happened to be made on cloth and not on paper. Improved machinery, easier dyes and simpler techniques did not necessarily improve design. Mass production and cost governed the products and not the older standards of craftsmanship. In common with those of the rest of Europe, in 1875 most French fabrics were poorly drawn, badly engraved and printed in harsh colours.

Since the beginning of this century screen printing has been extensively practised in France and has been used in the production of fabrics for the world of *haute couture* in conjunction with the technique of spraying dye through stencils by means of an air brush, for individual lengths and speciality dresses. This method has been of especial use to the fashion designers of Paris.

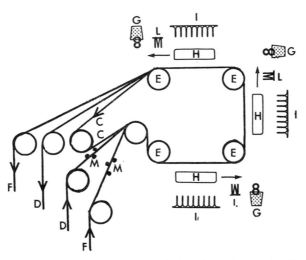

7. The Perrotine printing machine, 1834, for printing from flat blocks. The four rollers, E, carry an endless blanket C covered by a 'back grey' cotton fabric D, and then the fabric to be printed F. The colour pad H has to a and fro motion. It moves to the colour box G and on its return journey the brush L comes into operation and smooths out the colour on the pad. The printing block, I, now comes forward to receive the colour from the pad. The block recedes, as the pad resumes its journey to the colour box. Then the block comes forward to print on the fabric. After printing the fabric moves forward one repeat and the printing continues with second and other colours exactly registering one on the other. Tension rollers are shown at M.

The Art Nouveau style, called *Le Style Moderne* in France, was rampant from 1895 with the undulating forms and floral motifs that prevailed in the textile designs of Georges de Feure and Eugene Gaillard. These were sold in the new shop in Paris opened by Samuel Bing (b. 1838) in 1895 and called *L'Art Nouveau*, and another opened by Julius Meier-Graef in 1897 called *La Maison Moderne*. *Le Style Moderne* lasted until the early twenties.

Germany

Textile printing in Germany was centred mainly in the border areas stretching north from Basle. Here, as has already been mentioned, as well as to the north, Swiss manufacturers established a number of print works at Berlin, Konstanz, Mulhouse (in Alsace) and Lörrach, as well as others that grew up elsewhere, and particularly in Silesia. The Rhenish cloth-printing trade of the Middle Ages often used gold and silver prints on plain-coloured cloths, and examples of fourteenth- and fifteenth-century textiles showing this technique, but copying the patterns of brocades, are in Krefeld collections.

The calico trade had suffered a set-back in 1721 when Frederick William I protected the home weavers and dyers of wool and linen by forbidding the wearing, importing or selling of any kind of printed or painted calico. As in France, the decree was honoured more in the breach than in the observance and by 1743 print works were established in various parts; the regulations were relaxed in

1752 to allow printing, but not the import or wearing of foreign printed calicos and chintz.

At Augsburg in southern Germany a water-colour method similar to the Swiss application technique was developed by Jeremy Neuhofer in 1689. The following year he visited Holland to study the process of printing with fast colours.

In 1759 Johann Heinrich von Schule opened his print works, which was in existence until the early 1800s. He employed gold and silver in his printing on cloth, often upon coloured grounds.

Alois Senefelder (1772–1834) developed an interesting form of printing quite distinct from the accepted techniques at this period. He had already invented the method of printing called lithography. This technique employed the antipathy between grease and water by drawing the design (or background) in wax or grease on a slab of limestone, wetting the slab and rolling on an oil pigment or dye. This would take only on the waxed areas and would so print off the design (or background) on to a sheet of paper. Senefelder wished to adapt this technique to the printing of calico. Although his experiments did not lead to commercial production in his lifetime, the method was used at a later date in Augsburg and Alsace to print shawls and *mouchoirs* of silk and cotton.

Between 1815 and 1848 Germany and Austria were noted for a furnishing fashion usually named *Beidermeier*, after the name given to the middle classes in Germany at this time. In printed textiles this meant a design of flowers scattered over a plain background.

In the 1860s a copper-based pigment colour called Brunswick green was placed on the market, followed by Scheele's green and Schweinfurt or Paris green. These were all based on highly poisonous powdered metal salts and were frequently denounced and banned as toxic by the authorities. Stories were circulated of persons who had died by breathing in the powder brushed from ball dresses printed with the colours, and of poisoners who hung wall hangings and curtains so printed in the bedrooms and closets of their victims.

Textile printing followed the same pattern of development as in France and Switzerland during the nineteenth century, with many new patents and inventions in the field of textile machinery as well as in dye chemistry.

The first radical change in design came with the spread of the ideas of William Morris, and of the English Art and Crafts Movement and the Scottish pioneers. The culmination of these influences was seen in the publication of the magazines *Pan* in Berlin in 1895 and *Die Jugend* in Munich in 1896. These were the first indication of Art Nouveau, which became known in Germany as *Jugendstil*. The leader of the movement was Henri Van de Velde (1863–1957) and he and his followers were much influenced by William Morris and later by Charles Rennie Mackintosh and the Glasgow group. The printed textiles produced were typical of the movement, but the main effects were seen in weaving techniques and, as the work of other men including Mackmurdo, Sumner, Voysey and Ashbee became better known on the Continent, many German designers visited England to learn the latest ideas. Amongst them was Herman Muthesius, who, in 1907, formed the *Deutscher Werkbund*, an association of manufacturers, architects and craftsmen. By 1914 the architect Walter Gropius (1883–1969) had come to the forefront of the younger architect-designers. His belief that the artist possessed the power 'to breathe life into the dead product of the machine' made him the logical successor to Van de Velde when the latter resigned as Principal of the Weimar School of Art and Crafts.

This school had developed craft workshops in which were created 'a logical structure of products', as well as establishing links with local manufacturers. After a considerable period of discussion, spread over the disorganization and disillusion of World War I, Gropius was not only appointed Principal in 1919 but also given permission to change the name of the school to *das Staatliches Bauhaus*. He had refined his aims and ideals so as to offer a programme 'in which the artist would come to terms with the most powerful means of modern production, the machine, from the simplest tool to the most specialized machinery. Students would form the nucleus of a happy working community, such as had existed in an ideal way in the masons' lodges of the Middle Ages.'[1] The manifesto drew in an inspired collection of enthusiastic students. By appointing a number of staff—amongst whom were painters of the Expressionist group such as Paul Klee (1879–1940) and Wassily Kandinsky (1866–1944)—so as to obtain a combined process of teaching by two persons, one an artist and one a technician, he tried to fuse artistic inspiration with sound techniques. His manifesto further proclaimed: 'Let us create a new' guild of craftsmen, 'without the class distinctions which raise an arrogant barrier between craftsmen and artist.' This was a direct interpretation of the teaching of William Morris and other nineteenth-century pioneers. As such it caused much conflict in the logical development of a Bauhaus ideology.

The first workshop to be established was that for weaving, and by 1920 it numbered not only Klee and Georg Muche (b. 1895) among its artists but Gunta Stölzl and Hélène Börner among its technicians.

As other workshops were established it was necessary to form a core of designers, and the most radical basic design course was organized and run by Johannes Itten (1888–1967), who preached the direct involvement of the designer with the materials he was to use. 'This course is intended to liberate the student's creative power, to give him an understanding of nature's materials, and to acquaint him with the basic principles which underlie all creative activity in the visual arts.'[2]

Internal quarrels and external antagonism brought about the removal of the Bauhaus from Weimar to Dessau in 1925. Here the dual system of instruction was abolished. Anni Albers, Otti Berger and Lis Beyer joined Gunta Stölzl in the weaving workshops. After the resignation of Gropius in 1928 the Bauhaus carried on at first under the direction of Hannes Meyer (1889–1954) and then under Ludwig Mies van der Rohe (1886–1969), until the Nazis closed it down in

[1] Gropius W. *Memorandum to the Grand Duke of Saxe Weimar* 1914
[2] Brandford C. T. *Bauhaus Weimar* 1919–25, *Dessau* 1925–8, Boston 1952

1932. The reopened, but private, venture in Berlin suffered the same fate in 1933.

The Bauhaus has been covered at some length because, although no printed textiles were actually produced, the new approach to design had a revolutionary effect upon all succeeding designers of printed textiles and particularly the many who were Bauhaus students or were taught by such persons. The Bauhaus teachings greatly affected all the crafts in Europe other than Nazi Germany during the Art Deco period of the twenties and thirties. In printed textiles this influence often appeared as a basic cube-sphere-triangle form of pattern. This design form still reappears at regular intervals between other trends.

The general interest in abstract pattern that has developed particularly since World War II owes a great deal to the research and combined inspiration of the staff and students of the Bauhaus. It is difficult to appreciate how much the sources of pattern have changed following Gropius, Ittens and the non-representational schools of painting. The complicated abstract pattern of today is widely accepted at all levels of society and is also commercially profitable since the introduction of screen printing. It is unlikely that it would have become so widespread without the teachings of the Bauhaus.

India

The highest achievement in hand block-printed fabrics was undoubtedly reached in the field of Indian textiles up to the early nineteenth century. No other country has had such a long and continuous influence on the printed cloths of other countries and their economic and social development and aesthetics. It is known that the craft was practised as early as 400 BC (printing blocks are said to have been in existence dating back to 3000 BC). For many centuries prior to the European traders' first arrival in the Indies from the route around the Cape of Good Hope in 1498 there had been an extensive trade in a wide variety of goods, including painted and printed cottons, between India, China, Java and the Philippines. These were mainly exported from the ports of the Masulipatam and Coromandel coasts in the largest ships then known, as described by Marco Polo in the thirteenth century. Land routes also carried textiles from India as far as Egypt, Arabia, Turkistan, China, Siam and Java.

The actual word chintz, by which these cottons were so long known, is derived from a Hindu word, *chint*, which means coloured or variegated.

Other names mentioned by W. S. Hadoway include *chites, cheentes, chidneys, chinte, scrittones, pintado* and *salampores*. Originally it meant a cotton fabric printed or painted with fast colours. Now it refers to a glazed material.

The muslins in particular were so fine that old legends tell the story of Princess Zeb-un-Nissa, who appeared in public apparently wearing nothing. When her father rebuked her she replied that she had, in fact, seven layers of muslin wrapped around her. The names given to these fabrics were most evocative, and when translated become woven air (*bafthawa*) and evening dew (*shabnam*). The latter obtained its name because if laid wet on the grass, it was totally invisible. A Dr Taylor reported in 1846 that a pound of cotton thread contained about 250 miles in length. A Persian ambassador in the 1630s brought back a thirty-yard muslin turban so fine that it could be hardly be felt when touched. The secret of these Dacca muslins is now lost, but other fine *dorias* or striped muslins are still made in Acca, Gwalior, and other areas, as well as the *charkanas* or chessboard-patterned muslins and the *jamdani* with small sprig patterns.

It is probable that the development of the great skills found in the work of later Indian dyers, followed the pattern already described in the section on primitive methods. It is equally obvious that a good knowledge of the chemistry of vegetable dyes was developed at a very early period. Colours were not only brilliant and of great variety, they were also often exceedingly subtle and particularly so in their tonal qualities. Their colours seem to contain hidden qualities and effects that only appear in differing lights. The *pagris* or headwear produced in Rajasthan (originally Rajputana), Kotah and Alwar contained two slightly differing shades which produced a constantly changing colour pattern as the fabric rippled.

It is tragic that such a vast wealth of knowledge concerning the use of the indigenous dye materials has now dwindled to a few areas, in the face of the economic pressures brought in with foreign synthetic dyes and the establishment of European-style printing factories.

The various districts were noted for particular dyes and styles of dyeing. Bengal produced simple uniform shades with narrow contrasting borders; Assam was famed for its beautiful reds and Chinese blue; Punjab for brilliant yellows, magentas and purples; the mulberry (*Morinda tinctoria*) bark and roots of the Nagpur district gave superb rich deep reds or yellows; in Alwar and Kotar, of Rajathan, one side of the cotton was dyed yellow and the other red, or red and green, and without any merging of the colours. Such skill transcends virtuosity and can only be the outcome of continuous experiment over a long period by sensitive craftsmen.

Other dyes used in dyeing, painting and printing included *chay* from the roots of the Indian madder (*Oldenlandia umbellata*), which gave the rich, brilliant reds of the south; *chay* from the bark of brazil-wood (*Caesalpinia sappan*), giving reds, violets and deep brown, together with yellows from larkspur and saffron; oranges from jasmine, delphinium, carthamus; reds from cochineal, logwood and pistachio galls; purples from cochineal with indigo; greens from indigo with jasmine; blues from indigo; blacks from iron filings. At one time, a local difficulty in Kashmir occurred with greens and it was overcome by boiling the dye out of green baize cloth imported from England.

Our knowledge of the printed cottons is substantiated by many further accounts from earliest times. The records of the invasion of India by Alexander the Great in 327 BC describe the brilliant, printed cloths and, as has already been mentioned, the ruins of Fostat or old Cairo in Egypt have yielded a very large number of early Indian fabrics resist printed from blocks and dyed blue with indigo or red with madder.

Many Greek and Roman writers of the time of Christ referred to the growing Coromandel coast trade in patterned cottons. Chinese accounts by the travellers of Cheng-Ho of the fifteenth century mention Calicut-printed cottons. In the Company records of 1634–6 a white woollen cloth is mentioned, which was sent to India to be dyed by Charles I.

Duarte Barbosa, a Portuguese official in the sixteenth century, surveyed the cotton industry of India, the French voyager Francois Bernier in 1665 mentions the beautiful hand-painted chintz. These are only a few of our references, but it is likely that the main sources so far discovered are in three long and detailed documents.

The first is a manuscript of 333 pages still under detailed examination written between 1678 and 1680 and now known as the Roques Manuscript. It consists of a detailed account of the textile trade and manufacturing processes witnessed by the author, mainly at Ahmedabad, Burhanpur and Sironj. One fact that has emerged so far is that Indian craftsmen of that period did practise wood-block printing with treegum-thickened mordants and pigment colours.

The second is known as the Beaulieu Manuscript and dates to about 1734. It is quoted in a famous treatise on cotton painting by the Basle manufacturer Jean Ryhiner (1728–90) which was written in 1766 but not published until 1865, and in the Chevalier de Querelles's book *Traité sur les toiles peintes*, Paris 1760. It is in existence in Paris and contains eleven actual samples of painted cloth brought back by a naval officer, M. de Beaulieu, as well as full details of the processes used.

The third was written by Father Coeurdoux, a missionary of the Company of Jesus, who described the method of decoration of cottons in letters dated 1742 and 1747 from the East Indies to his superiors in Europe. He described how the cloth was bleached and mordanted by the use of an extract of a dry fruit called cadou and buffalo milk. The design was applied by pouncing ground charcoal through a perforated paper pattern. This design was then brush-lined or filled in with a black iron dye and a red dye. It was protected where necessary with a wax resist and dyed blue with indigo. The wax was then removed by steeping in boiling water and the background cloth re-bleached and prepared again for a red dyeing. This was followed by more waxing and mordanting and the red dyeing. Further stripping, bleaching of the remaining ground and preparation of the fabric for re-dyeing was necessary, and a rather impermanent yellow applied by brush over blue to produce green, or direct on to the ground white for yellow. A type of brush was made from bamboo and cloth. The end of a piece of bamboo was pointed and slit, and a piece of cloth inserted. This was soaked in dye and formed a reservoir which was squeezed to obtain the necessary flow of dye. A similar implement was used to apply the wax.

Father Coeurdoux's actual descriptions contain many further processes in the printing and the dye preparation and these were studied and commented upon by Edward Bancroft (1744–1821), the distinguished English chemist, in his book *Experimental researches concerning the philosophy of permanent colours*, London 1794 and 1813. It was also used in G. P. Baker's outstanding work *Calico painting and printing in the East Indies in the 17th and 18th centuries*, London 1921, and in a number of Continental books and journals of the seventeenth and eighteenth centuries.

In India textiles have always been one facet of a complex ritual of life rather than a reflection of a current trend or fashion. It was against a background of innumerable invasions from peoples with their own virile cultures and religions that India gradually fashioned her own pattern of hereditary guilds organized within rigid caste systems and bound by rigid tribal laws. As one link in an unbroken ethos, the craftsman came to resist outside attempts to alter his wish to renew in each generation the traditions of the past. Each ethnic group preserved its own characteristics, its own dyes, ways of dyeing and designs. The centre of village textile design was the religious tradition. Only that which was perfect was fit for the temple, and since all life was governed by ritual, so all textiles must be perfect. In time each process, such as that of the weaver, block-cutter, printer, dye-mixer and the other necessary stages, became the work of separate groups of *chiltas* or craftsmen, who spent their whole lives at one particular technique.

The textiles were of five main types which we would now describe as painted; tied and dyed; resist printed with wax or starch from blocks and then dyed; direct printed with a dye paste from a block and lastly stencil printed (either with a resist or with a dye paste).

The earliest specimen of resist-dyed cotton cloth dates back to the eighth century AD. It is only from carvings and sculpture that we can learn of earlier patterns. The fragments discovered in the tombs of Fostat in Egypt and in central Asian cities by Sir Aurel Stein have been dated as twelfth century and were printed in Gujerat.

The main colour belt of India coincides with the main printing belt and extends from the interior of Sindh through the deserts of Cutch, Kathiawar and Rajutana to Gujerat. The variations in design and technique were innumerable. Whole villages existed purely to prepare cloths for export.

The European merchants who imported these painted and printed fabrics in the sixteenth and seventeenth centuries, through the various East India Companies, found that the Indian craftsmen, although so skilled in the designing and making of calicoes, lacked any power of organization and planning to meet the large-scale production necessary to satisfy the great demand. Despite the establishment by the companies of warehouses, manufactories and forts, the Indians would not change their traditional methods just to please foreigners. If they had done so, then India might still be a country famed for its present production of printed textiles. The inability to adapt to demand, coupled with the European import prohibitions and the dawning in the West of a mechanized age of machine spinning and roller printing created a rival with which the Indian hand craftsmen could not compete. At various times attempts were made to establish

European manufactories in India. The late Peter Floud, of the Victoria and Albert Museum, discovered a petition addressed to the House of Commons in 1782 by a group of cotton importers concerning the establishment of such a print works with copper plates and other machinery imported from England under the auspices of the East India Company, much to the alarm of the English importers. A pattern book of the Company of the early 1800s lists 906 different printed cloths from only three districts.

Mrs Annie Besant (1847–1933), President of the Theosophical Society, also encouraged such a print works at the beginning of this century in an attempt to re-establish rural industries.

The East India Companies and the Indian calico printers were at great pains to discover the wishes of their customers. Representatives visited both Europe and India to discover the latest patterns, send samples back and obtain cheap copies. At times, the inability of one culture to understand the conventions of another culture led to strange inconsistencies in designs. Eastern peoples often find the Western idea of perspective in pictures incomprehensible, so any errors in the drawings copied from the designs of English printers and sent back to be copied in India were often faithfully reproduced. Hands appear growing out of legs, the trunk of a Tree of Life design was suddenly cut off to reappear as a small twig, half a rabbit was strangely joined to half a bird. As well as dress fabrics, many other textiles were produced, such as bedspreads and quilts, bed curtains, wall hangings, curtains, upholstery and floor coverings. Pepys, in his diary entry for 5 September 1663, wrote 'Bought my wife a chint, that is, a painted East Indian callico for to line her new study.' Evelyn, on 30 December 1665: 'I supped at my Lady Mordaunt's, where was a roome hung with Pintado, full of figures, prettily representing sundry trades and occupations of the Indians with their habits.' An unknown writer in 1682 obviously knew a universal truth 'everyone desires something that their neighbours have not the like'. The nature of hand-painted or printed designs was bound to please such a wish which could never be satisfied by a machine-printed design. 'The brilliance and cleanly appearance of the glazed and shining cloths' was remarked upon by Queen Mary, who hung her own bed and rooms with them. This caused Defoe to write in 1772 in his *Tour through Great Britain* that she 'brought the love of Fine East-India Callicoes such as were then called Massalapatan, Chintes, Atlasses [the name for a then fashionable bed] . . . which after descended into the Humour of the Common People so much as to make them grievous to our Trade and Ruining to our manufacture'. The continued demand for Indian fabrics led to a number of import restrictions until they were totally banned in 1700.

The great skills of the village craftsman gave way to the cheapest mechanical forms of weaving, printing and dyeing on inexpensive fabrics often called bazaar cloths. These bore little resemblance to the original designs and became more and more crude in cutting and planning. This development was forced upon Indian centres where the finest prints had been produced, by the flooding of the Indian markets with very cheap English cotton prints imitating old Indian styles at a period when the Indian fabrics were prohibited in England. In order to compete with these so-called Manchester prints, many of the original centres of printing disappeared, and new centres appeared to produce cheap block-printed cloths. The largest of these still in operation is at Farrukhabad in Uttar Pradesh, south of Delhi, which produces a vast quantity of Indian prints for export to Europe and America. State control is imposed to obtain standards of quality and fastness, but the low price asked for these fabrics must leave little profit for the Indian *chipa* or fabric printer (see plate 5).

After World War II a resurgence in printed textiles took place with the introduction of reactive dyestuffs and modern machinery. Unfortunately the designs were not rethought, but adapted from the older forms with little feeling or understanding. This also applied to the majority of the Western-style prints.

There seems little solution feasible at the present time. Unemployment has grown in the hand printing industry to such large proportions as to threaten the whole tradition of a way of life for a large section of the population. Despite official encouragement in the use of older techniques to produce specialized work in printed textiles, it has not been possible to resist the impositions of mass patterns of machine culture in a country with such economic problems as India.

An excellent museum of the traditional fabrics of India has been established at Ahmedabad, called the Calico Museum of Textiles. Various bodies such as the All India Handicrafts Board and the Indian Co-operative Union are concerned extensively with the continuance of inherited techniques and the finest national designs.

From the richness of inspiration that other countries have derived from the work of Indian designers, two examples may be selected for individual attention.

The first is the famed Paisley pattern. Originally, this cone or seed-pod unit was a symbol of life and fertility many thousands of years before the birth of Christ. It is likely that it originated in ancient Persia, where it is found in the patterns on the costumes and furnishings of the persons and households represented by frescoes, carvings, sculptures and tomb remains. This unit was developed as a speciality of the province of Kashmir, which lay high above sea-level in the north-west of India at the edge of the Himalayas. The woven shawls of this district bore embroidered patterns based on the cone shape, and since the area was across the path of the main land trade routes from Persia to the west and south, their fame spread far during the thirteenth and fourteenth centuries. The unit itself was of such a flexible and basic nature that it was readily adapted to block printing, and has since become a most established and universally accepted design in all forms of textiles.

The word Paisley gradually supplanted the original Kashmir, as the name given to this type of pattern, after a Mr Paterson of the weaving town of Paisley in Scotland first succeeded in weaving an imitation Indian shawl with the popular design around 1800. He was fortunate in that the weavers of Paisley had already worked in silk, gauze, fine lawn and damask and had obtained a reputation as good as, or even superior to, that of the famed weavers of Spitalfields. Although they possessed the skill and knowledge to obtain the appearance and feel of a genuine Kashmir product it took a great deal of experiment over a number of years, using local themes as pattern sources, before they produced versions closely based on the Kashmir style. They were helped in this by improvements to the draw-loom they used; by the general acceptance of the Jacquard loom (although invented in 1801 it was not used extensively in Scotland until around 1850); by the development of the French thread which spun wool yarn around a silk cone, and by royal patronage, which did much to popularize the Paisley Pine, as the unit was now called, to attain the supreme height of fashion between 1850 and 1860.

Despite the overwhelming demand the manufacturers found that the products were too costly for the masses. A Scottish shawl took a week to produce, an Indian original could take up to three years, but if a printed version could be made that still looked and felt like a woven shawl then each shawl would only take a few minutes to print and show a good profit at a tenth of the price. Using plain, well-proven fabric, the market was soon flooded with varying qualities of printed shawls from cashmere to fine wool, silk gauze to silk twill. However, as a result the demand fell off and the industry declined. An early example of the dangers of mass production.

The basic pattern unit persisted, although by now it had developed from the original Indian design to a long, elongated and fantastic scroll form which still carried the mystic quality of the Orient. It still continues as one of the few permanent and recognizable complex sources of inspiration used by designers, and although no longer a dominant selling line, has a steady market.

Other relevant Indian pattern units of the same form were the mango patterns popular in many widely separated areas, the *kalka* patterns which were particularly developed in the Madras and other areas and the Persian Pear patterns used in rug decoration. This was a fundamental pattern form in Persian textiles, where, from the third century, the palm tree became identified with the second example of Indian influence upon other forms of designs, the Indian Tree of Life, the *homa*. In printed textiles it was usually recognizable as a tree, whereas in woven fabrics it often became a stylized form such as a rod surrounded by stars. The tree itself changed to the shape of the trees growing in a particular area such as the cypress, pine, palm or mulberry (see plate 7).

In ancient Babylonia designs of twin griffins with a palm tree between them were common. In the Old Testament two trees are mentioned, but whereas the West adopted the Tree of Knowledge the East took the Tree of Life from its own legends. It was believed to bear fruits which conveyed eternal life. Since it was symbolic, its representation was invariably stylized. In the West the Tree of Knowledge was always treated realistically. Little is known of the transition in the design of the tree from the early Sassanian silks to its most involved and fantastic development in Indian textiles of the seventeenth and eighteenth centuries. Here it usually appears as a large tree growing from a rocky hillock, often with a fountain of life flowing from a cleft in the tree or the rock. The curved branches of the tree bear long lancet-shaped leaves and extremely large ornate flowers. Among the branches exotic birds perch and flutter while small animals play between the roots or around ornamental flower vases that are sometimes placed on either side of the tree trunk. All is usually contained within a rectangular border of formalized flower garlands (see plate 6).

John Irwin and K. B. Brett have both discussed the results of recent research as to whether this was an entirely Indian conception. They favour the view that it was a compound of Chinese, European and Indian influences. It would seem that the first entirely Indian Tree of Life chintz patterns brought to Europe were too foreign for European tastes and so the companies sent out pattern books of acceptable designs for the Indian chintz painters to copy or adapt. These were based upon current European fashions and so a hybrid form grew up of exotic decoration based upon a realistic European foundation. Influences can be traced of Western chintz designers, lace and embroidery patterns as well as the original Indian forms. As has been mentioned, it is obvious that persons of an Eastern culture have attempted to literally translate patterns of another, Western, culture, often with incongruous results.

Although similar decorations on a smaller scale exist such as the *stupa*-shaped Persian designs or architectural forms based upon mosque doorways, the majority of these *kalamkars* or *palampores* were very large and 12 ft × 8 ft was a quite common size. They were exceedingly popular and were exported to Europe through the English, French and Dutch East India Companies to be used as hangings or bed coverings. Sir George Birdwood said of them: 'In point of art decoration they are simply incomparable. As art works they are to be classed with the finest Indian pottery and the grandest carpets' (see plate 8).

Upon close examination all the painted areas display exquisite detail and colour. When it is considered that each of the finer *palampores* was entirely executed by hand and involved a 'stencilling' or pouncing of the design, hand painting and possibly the printing of small blocks, as well as all the other preparing, bleaching processes described, and that it could take many months to complete it is possible to appreciate their relative high cost. The individuality of such work made them so desirable to Europeans that they were prepared to pay, although the actual Indian craftsman received little reward for his skilled and devoted labours.

Italy

Apart from the trading posts and print works established by the Swiss in parts of northern Italy, as already mentioned—the earlier wood-block printing that produced the Tapestry of Sion of the fourteenth century and the works around Venice and Florence—a considerable number of *mezzari* or *meseri* veils for covering the head and shoulders of peasant women were printed in the Genoa area in the late seventeenth century and up until about 1855. These were printed from wood blocks on cotton material imported from other European countries. The industry was commenced by a Swiss, Michele Speich, from Glarus in 1787 at Conegliano and Campi, just outside Genoa. Luigi Teston worked at San Pier d'Arena from 1830. The earlier patterns were copied from *indiennes* and were bright and strong in colour. Later the colours became rather insipid. In Paris such fabrics were known as *toiles de Gênes*.

At the present day a number of designers and textile printers are working with the screen printing of lengths and individual tourist items, such as scarves. Many of these are of high design and particularly those from the firms of Ornella Noorda, Locatex s.r.l., Manifattura J.S.A., and Fede Cheti.

Netherlands and Belgium

The Dutch merchants and explorers were some of the first to bring back the painted and printed Coromandel cloths from the East during the early seventeenth century. The Dutch East India Company was founded in 1602 to ensure the advantages obtained from co-operative trading. The heavy Spanish costume common at that time gave way to the more exotic Eastern cloths, and Dutch textile printers attempted to imitate the brilliantly coloured Indian cottons which were not only fast to water but became more beautiful and brilliant when washed. Their first attempts with the oil or water colours long used in Europe, that either smelt badly or would not wash, bore no comparison with the Eastern cloths printed or painted with mordant dyes and indigo.

The first European print works was founded at Amersfoort in Holland in 1678 and attempted to use Indian methods. Amsterdam with its port and trading facilities attracted many other calico print works and other countries sent their printers there to learn the trade. At the same time Dutch printers journeyed to other countries and records show their presence in England (in 1710), in Switzerland, France and Germany.

By the second half of the eighteenth century Dutch printers had succeeded in copying the sheer Asiatic cottons by using copper plates. French competition from Oberkampf, English from Peel and German from Schüle, together with the economic and import restrictions imposed by various countries, gradually reduced the number of print shops, until after the separation of Belgium and Holland in 1830 only a few large print works were left, in Haarlem and Leyden, to form the basis of an industry that dealt in the main with the export trade to the Dutch colonies. As has already been described, much of this was in the batik style made so popular by the Indonesian fabrics.

Factories were also established in overseas ports or possessions, including India, Java, Sumatra, Ceylon and the Moluccas.

Russia

A development from the traditional craft of icon painting took place during the sixteenth century when wood blocks were used to print vegetable colours on coarse linen known as *noboyka*. Since icon painters were itinerant journeymen who travelled from village to village practising their craft, it is thought likely that the fabric printers would do the same. They fulfilled the immediate needs of the home and their floral, geometrical or pictorial themes arose directly from the techniques of wood cutting and a close observation of nature. Oil-bound pigments were also used. These techniques continued to the eighteenth century, when the first Russian *indienne* manufactory was established at Krasnoe Selo near St Petersburg (now Leningrad) by two Englishmen in 1755 (see plate 19).

A number of cloth-printing shops were established near Moscow in 1780 and in 1799 in Moscow itself.

An interesting technique was the production of *dymka* cloths. In this method damped and unbleached linen was printed with blocks which had been first blackened with soot from the smoke of burning linseed and then coated with colour. The linen was then made into skirts. The prints were fast to rubbing and light, but not to water (see plate 17).

In the late nineteenth century a fair number of French and German technicians did work in Russian factories, one of the most eminent being the firm of Zündee in Moscow. The prints were of a similar design, but not of the standard of the more conservative European factories at that time. L. Diserens, who worked in this factory and that of Manufacture des trois Montagues Prochoraff before 1917, lists other works in his own books. These two factories are now thought to be renamed 1-ja.S.N.F. and Trekhgornja Manufacture respectively.

Scandinavia

Denmark, Finland, Norway and Sweden, although diverse and independent countries in many ways, still possess a many-sided common culture and in no craft was this exemplified as in textiles. All four countries, after a fairly conformist policy up to World War II, suddenly united in a great breakthrough in colour and design that swept through the rest of Europe and persists to the present day. The clear, clean, brilliant and unusual hues, together with bold, dramatic, geometrical shapes provided such a natural relief from the grey glumness of the war years that the whole form of textile designing was changed. Small print shops were established which grew into well-organized small factories still organized on the individual craftsman basis contained within a co-operative selling organization. The book *Scandinavian Domestic Design* by Erik

Zahle contains a list of short biographies of many craftsmen in Scandinavia who practise textile printing and designing.

In Finland, in particular, much good, typically Finnish design has been produced by Marimekko Oy; Porin Puuvilla Oy; E. Helenius Oy; Tampella and another firm printing on non-woven rayon fabric Oy Suonen Vanulehdas-Finnwad Ltd. Their work is designed by such designers as Marjalüsa Lipasti; Marjatta Metsovaara; Maija Isola; Raili Konttinen; Talvikki Talvitie and Timo Sarpaneva.

Spain

The first Spanish calico print works were established by Esteban Canals in Barcelona in 1738. In common with other European manufacturers of the period, this copied the *indiennes* and used the imported Eastern textiles as a source of pattern. This industry also helped the newly established Catalonian cotton mills. The textile-dyeing trade had progressed beyond the ancient guild system and researched extensively into the cultivation and use of such dyes as madder.

As well as cotton printing, there also developed a silk-printing industry, the products of which were exported in large quantities to the Spanish South American colonies.

The War of Independence against Napoleon caused the destruction of most of the Catalonian textile industry by 1815. Its later rebuilding did not stress the printing aspects.

Switzerland

Switzerland benefited from the freedom given to its calico printers as contrasted with the punitive restrictions imposed in many other European countries. Textile printing developed in certain definite areas usually circumscribed geographically within valleys and plains separated by mountains or rivers.

The first two print works were founded in Geneva in 1687 and 1689 and engaged printers from Lyons. The most famous manufacturer was Jean-Solomon Fazy (1709–82) who had studied calico printing in Holland and soon established his own print works as a centre of calico printing to which came textile printers, block designers and manufacturers from many countries who wished to study the latest developments. He excelled in the superb indigo-blue prints called *indiennes* which poured out of his factories in profusion, to be sold in Italy, southern France (despite the ban on imports until 1759), Spain and Portugal. With other manufacturers, including the Petit family, he brought great prosperity to Geneva until France imposed high duties upon *indiennes* in 1785. The Revolution followed the annexation of Geneva by France and Napoleon's continental blockade, so that by the 1830s, the Genevan print industry had almost entirely vanished.

In Zürich, a method of printing in water-colours called 'application' printing had early taken the place of the oil-colour pigment method which still persisted in the rest of Europe. In this water-colour technique the colour used contained both the dye and the fixing agent in combination. It had the advantage of being of use on silk and linen as well as on cotton. Although not particularly fast, the colours were cheap and easy to print. They remained in favour until the late nineteenth century.

The original print works in Zürich seems to have employed Dutch dyers around 1701. The first well-known manufacturer of *indiennes* is thought to have been David Esslinger (1679–1750), who started to print in 1720, and by the 1750s Esslinger handkerchiefs, printed on both sides with matching designs, were well known. Turkey red dyeing also developed in this area and the new Esslinger print works on the Limmat river, built in 1780, not only employed this method to dye its cotton cloths a dark red before printing on them, but gradually established a model factory. Again, taxes imposed in 1834 by the German Customs Union caused most factories in Zürich to close.

In Berne the industry was established in 1706, with a large number of small print works producing highly elaborate patterns with flowers, fruits, butterflies, birds and other natural subjects in many colours and printed, in the main, in water-colours. This industry, too, could not weather the economic restrictions imposed by France in 1785. In Basle, Samuel Ryhiner (1696–1757) opened his first calico works in 1716 and around 1750 both Oberkampf senior and Oberkampf junior worked in one of his factories.

The most important areas, however, were to be the cantons of Neuchâtel in the West in the eighteenth century, and Glarus in the East in the nineteenth century. The former adopted the roller-printing techniques in the industry founded by the wealthy Huguenots who had settled there in the seventeenth century. Unlike the manufacturers in other areas, the manufacturers of Neuchâtel left the sale of the cloths to merchants and themselves concentrated upon the actual printing. This employment of a specialist on both sides undoubtedly contributed to the rapid growth of the industry. By 1800 the print works at Cortaillod had developed into the largest calico print works in Switzerland, exporting plain red prints, illuminated cloths, blue lapis styles, Turkey red headsquares, printed dress materials and wall coverings to Italy, France, Belgium and North America. After many years of fluctuating trade that suffered from French and German restrictions, the industry finally closed down in 1875. Without doubt, its work was not as good as the outstanding work of the Jouy factories, but its 'madder' styles in particular were of a very high level.

In 1714 cotton spinning was introduced into the canton of Glarus; Johann Heinrich Streiff (1709–80) established the first calico printing works there in 1740. Here were produced *indiennes*, *persiennes* and *mouchoirs*, all of which were mainly wax or paste resists on an indigo-blue ground with geometrical and stylized flower designs. Other works rapidly followed until by the 1840s Glarus was renowned for its wide variety of printed cloths. Machine printing was introduced in the 1860s and also Perrotine printing for coloured discharges on Turkey red dyed cloths.

One of the most noted houses was that of P. Blumer and Jenny, who not only worked a factory at Schwanden, but also owned a trading outlet in Italy which had become one of the main markets for Swiss fabrics both as a consuming country and as a step to the markets of the Near East. For these latter markets Blumer and Jenny produced the exceedingly popular Yasma patterns of extremely delicate black or brown outlines with many inserted colours.

By World War I the protective policies adopted by most European countries had so far reduced a once thriving-industry that only a few factories remained to print Manchester-type cloths for West Africa, together with some of the more specialized forms of printing upon silk, wool and pile fabrics.

At the present time screen printing and exclusive hand methods are used to produce finely woven printed cottons, African prints, flock prints and similar speciality forms in the Glarus and a few other areas.

The United States

A number of wood blocks of the early eighteenth century, now in the Memorial Hall in Deerfield, Massachusetts, are the earliest evidence of textile printing in the United States. They show strong Far Eastern influences in the patterns and are reflected in early samples of white and blue printed calico also in existence. It is likely that the original Dutch and German settlers on the east coast and particularly in Pennsylvania brought these skills with them. The earliest blocks would presumably copy traditional European designs and could be carved in a hardwood such as box, pear, sycamore, etc. The dyes were usually vegetable dyes in reds and blues and the articles ranged from handkerchiefs, squares, and clothing fabrics to bedspreads and furnishing materials.

The famous *toiles de Jouy* provided the inspiration for a number of the late eighteenth-century designs. It is known that there was quite a substantial import into the eastern states of French, English and Swiss calicoes and other printed goods. The printers we still know, such as the Englishman, John Hewson, who settled in Philadelphia in 1774, and the German, Herman Vandausen, who was printing Indian-style fabrics in Rhode Island at the end of the eighteenth century, derived much of their work from European and Oriental fabrics brought in in ever-increasing quantities. Martha Washington is reported to have worn dresses made from fabric printed by Hewson. The use of wooden blocks was gradually replaced in the mid-nineteenth century by etched copper rolls which led to the mass production era of the second half of the century. As in Europe, the original homespun efforts of local craftsmen, which had a fresh, spontaneous appeal, gave way to more sophisticated but often poorly designed and crudely etched designs in garish colours intended for the widest possible market at the lowest prices obtainable. The extremes of fashion that swept continental Europe during this period were not so prevalent in America, where a strong classical tradition, linked with the austere Puritanism that still survived there, restricted the influence of Paris to small avant-garde circles in the larger cities.

In 1780 Anna Doolittle of New Haven used copper plates to print patterns on her customers' own calico and linen. This printing of supplied cloth was quite common in America and Europe. In America, however, many housewives did their own printing, using local vegetable dyes and crudely cut wood-block patterns. In other areas the works developed as co-operatives. Many of these smaller firms printed in dark brown pigment colours upon cotton, fustian and other mixture fabrics.

In 1823 one of the most important cotton-printing factories in New England was the Taunton Massachusetts Manufacturing Company, who had their own village with spinning, weaving and printing mills each with its cottages and smithies and producing between fifteen hundred and two thousand printed pieces weekly. Much of this was intended for the southern trade and was bought by plantation-owners for their slaves.

Around 1830 stencils were often employed by journeymen artists who travelled from house to house and undertook all kinds of redecoration and minor repairs. They applied stencil patterns to walls, floors, ceilings, furniture and also plain cloth. Examples of the outstanding stencilled bedspreads of the nineteenth century may be seen in the American Museum in Claverton Manor, Bath.

One great silk family who produced woven and printed silk fabrics in the nineteenth century was Cheney Bros, the Cheney Silk Co, founded in 1838.

Apart from European influences, both of imported textiles and the craft traditions brought in by immigrants, such as the paper-cut designs from Poland, the designers and craftsmen were quick to use local sources of pattern. The south-western part of the United States shows a strong regional influence from the early Spanish colonists of New Mexico as well as the original pueblo Indian motifs; Red Indian sources can be traced in the work of craftsmen in the northern lakes areas and where the tribes settled along the eastern seaboard. In Pennsylvania the German and Swiss refugee craftsmen developed a form of design often called 'Dutch', which was really a corruption of *Deutsch* or German, and used gay colours and strong simple motifs.

Apart from a few artist craftsmen who continued to produce block-printed fabrics up to World War II, most textiles printed commercially employed either roller printing or screen printing. This last technique has been substantially developed in the States and many artists and designers have been attracted to it.

The designs follow the general trend of European design of the equivalent period. For an original approach to design, the work of the present-day group of weavers in the U.S.A. working on hangings and constructions is worth close examination.

APPENDICES

I Notes and references for further reading

Only books in English are given here unless the text in another language is of exceptional value. In the main they relate to printed textiles, although where pattern form is of value a number include woven cloths.

EARLY TECHNIQUES AND MATERIALS USED IN DYEING AND PRINTING

CIBA Reviews—Particularly numbers 8, 11, 12, 29, 30, 37, 41, 43, 49, 52, 54, 63, 70, 81, 98, 133, 136, 1962/5, 1967/1, 1968/2

D'Harcourt R. *Textiles of Ancient Peru and their Techniques* University of Washington Press, Seattle, 1962 (mainly woven textiles)

Forbes R.J. *Studies in Ancient Technology Textiles* Volume IV, E.J. Brill, Leiden, Netherlands, 1964. An excellent, concise summary of our present knowledge of the history of textile fibres, their spinning and processing and the tools used in spinning and weaving. It has most valuable and copious references to guide the reader to essays written by experts. It only contains a few paragraphs on the earlier known examples of block prints, it does contain considerable and detailed information upon dyestuffs, many of which were in constant use up to the development of synthetic dyestuffs in the mid 1800s

Forrer R. *Die Zeugdrucke der byzantinischen, romanischen, gotischen und späteren Kunstepochen.* Strasbourg, 1894 (in German)

Forrer R. *Die Künst des Zeugdrucks vom Mittelaltes bis zur Empirezeit* Strasbourg, 1898 (The Art of Calico Printing)

Kybalova L. *Coptic Textiles* Hamlyn, London, 1967 (woven textiles)

Lucas A. *Ancient Egyptian Materials and Industries* London, 1962

Pfister R. and Bellinger L. *Textiles* Yale University Press 1946

Thurstan V. *A Short History of Ancient Decorative Textiles* The Favil Press, London, 1954 (particularly woven textiles)

BARK, BAST OR TAPA CLOTH

Brigham W.T. „*Ka Hana Kapa*" a monograph of the Bishop Museum of Polynesian Ethnology, 1911 (detailed study of the bark cloths of Oceania, profusely illustrated in black and white, and colour. Out of print, but in large libraries)

CIBA Reviews—Particularly numbers 33 and 1965/1

Cranstone B.A.L. *Melanesia* British Museum, London, 1961, pp 55/56

Rattray. *Religion and Art in Ashanti* Oxford University Press, London, 1927 (some illustrations of Adinkira cloths as well as a very full account of general crafts)

Trowell M. *African Design* Faber & Faber, London, 1960 (very good account of all forms of African craftwork and design including bark cloth)

BATIK—WAX RESIST

Baker W.D. and I.S. *Batik and other Pattern Dyeing* Atkinson Mentzer and Co, Chicago, 1920

CIBA Reviews—Particularly numbers 58 and 1967/4

Furnival J.S. The Weaving and Batik Industries of Java *Asiatic Review* Volume XXXIII, No. 110, 1936

Haddon A.C. and Start L.E. *Iban or Sea Dayak Fabrics* Cambridge University Press, 1936 (also includes tie and dye and other crafts)

Irwin J. and Murphy R. *Batik* V. and A., H.M.S.O., London, 1969

Keller I. *Batik the Art and Craft* Charles E. Tuttle Company, U.S.A., 1966 (simplified history and excellent recipes)

Langewis L. and Wagner F.A. *Decorative Art in Indonesian Textiles* van der Peet, Amsterdam. F. Lewis, England, 1964 (an outstanding book, illustrated in black and white, with a good text and references)

Leur J.C. Van. *Indonesian Trade and Society* Van Hoeve, The Hague, 1955

Lewis A.B. *Javanese Batik Designs from Metal Stamps* Field Museums of Natural History, Chicago, 1924 (illustrations of prints from stamps)

Loebèr J.A. *Das Batiken. Eine Blüte indonesischen Kunstlebens* Oldenburg, 1926 (in German)

Mijer P. *Batiks and How To Make Them* Dodd, Mead and Company, New York, 1919 (recipes and good historical account of American batiks of the period)

Munsterberg O. *Chinesische Kunstgeschichte* Esslungen, 1924 (in German)

Primitive Staff musterungen Museum für Volkerkunde, Basel, 1963. et seq (in German; well illustrated catalogue)

Sammlungs-katalog No. 2, Extra-European Textiles Museums Bellerive Sammlung des Kunstgewerbemuseums, Zürich, N.D. (in German; well illustrated catalogue)

Soetopo S. (Ed) *Batik*, No. 9, Education and Culture Bureau of Issues, Balai Pustaka. 11/2 Bjl. Wahidin, Djakarta, Indonesia, 1957 (full of information, although the translation has to be read to be believed)

Steinmann A. *Batik. A Survey of Batik Design* F. Lewis, England, 1958 (a standard work upon the subject)

Torii R. *Artistic Designs used by the Miao-tze Tribe* Kokka No. 186, pp. 151 et seq, 1905

Tôyei S. *An Illustrated Catalogue of the Imperial Treasury called Shôsôin at Nara* Tokyo, 1910

Wagner, S.A. *Indonesia. Art of an Island Group* Methuen, London, 1962

BATIK—STARCH RESIST

CIBA Reviews—Particularly numbers 58 and 1967/4

Cole F.C. *The Wild Tribes of Davao District, Mindanas*, pp 154/5 Chicago, 1913

Fei C. and others. *Indigo Prints of China* Foreign Languages Press, Peking, 1956

Nigeria, No. 14, 1938, pp 125/129, 'Yoruba Pattern Dyeing'; No. 30, 1949, p 325, 'Art on the Drying Field'; No. 32, 1949, pp 41/47, 'Tiv Pattern Dyeing'; No. 54, 1957, pp 208/225, 'Yoruba Pattern Dyeing' (these articles also deal with tie and dyeing techniques)

Trowell M. *African Design* Faber and Faber, London, 1960 (well illustrated and good text on a wide variety of crafts)

Vydra J. *Indigo Blue Print in Slovak Folk Art* Artia, Prague, 1954 (a most useful account of early printing with oil colours and starch resists)

DISCHARGE METHODS

Clouzot H. *Tissues Negres* Paris N.D.

Kale D.G. *Principles of Cotton Printing* Bombay, 1957 (covers a number of these and other printing techniques)

Trowell M. *African Design* Faber and Faber, London, 1960

FIBRES AND TECHNIQUES

CIBA Reviews—Particularly numbers 95, 97, 99, 111, 114, 116, 118, 123, 127, 129, 130, 137, 141, 1961/3, 1962/2, 1962/5, 1962/6, 1963/5, 1964/4, 1964/6, 1965/1, 1965/2, 1965/3, 1966/2, 1967/2, 1968/2

Cook J.G. *Handbook of Textile Fibres* Merrow Publishing Co. Watford, 4th edit. 1968

Emery I. *The Primary Structures of Fabrics* The Textile Museum, Washington, D.C., 1966 (comprehensive account with an excellent bibliography)

Hill R. (Ed) *Fibres from Synthetic Polymers* Elsevier Publishing Co, London, 1953

Identification of Textile Materials The Textile Institute, 10 Blackfriars Street, Manchester 3

Index to Man Made Fibres of the World Harlequin Press, 3rd edit. 1967

Kornreich E. *Introduction to Fibres and Fabrics* Heywood Books, 2nd edit. 1966

Matthews J.M. *Textile Fibers* Ed. H. R. Mauersberger, John Wiley and Sons Inc. New York, 1954

Moncrieff R.W. *Man-made Fibres* Heywood Books, John Wiley and Sons Inc. New York, 4th edit. 1963

Onions W.J. *Wool, An Introduction to its Properties, Varieties, Uses and Production* Ernest Benn, London. 1962

Rankin W.M. and Hildreth E.M. *Textiles in the Home* Allman and Son, London, 1966

Thomson H. *Fibres and Fabrics of Today* Heinemann Educational Books Ltd, London, 1967

DYES, DYEING AND CHEMICALS

Before 1750

CIBA Reviews—Particularly numbers 4, 7, 9, 39, 68, 85

Colbert J.B. and D'Albo. *Instruction generale pour la teinture des laines et manufactures de laine de toutes couleurs et pour la culture des drogues ou ingrediens qu'on y employe* Paris, 1671 (in French, the set of regulations published by the French Comptroller General Jean Baptiste Colbert (1619–1683) to control dyes and dyeing in France which brought about the establishment of the great dyeing industry in France)

Hellot J. *L'art de la teinture des laines, et des etoffes de laine, en grande et petit teint, avec une instruction sur les debouilles* Paris, 1750 (in French, in English 1789 and 1901)

Leggett W.F. *Ancient and Medieval Dyes* Chemical Publishing Company, NY, 1944

Rosetti G. *Plictho de larte de tentori che insegna tenger pani telle banbasi et sede si per larthe magiore come per la commone* Venice, 1540 (in Italian, the first printed book on dyeing and a standard work of reference until the end of the seventeenth century)

After 1750

Blackshaw and Brightman R. *Dictionary of Dyeing and Textile Printing* George Newnes, London, 1961

Chaptal J.A.C. *L'art de la teinture du coton en rouge* Paris, 1807 (in French, the first concise presentation of the special difficulties encountered in the dyeing of cotton)

CIBA Reviews—Particularly numbers 115, 120, 128, 139, 140, 1961/2, 1964/2, 1965/5–6, 1966/3, 1969/1

Cockett S.R. and Hilton K.A. *Basic Chemistry of Textile Colouring and Finishing* National Trade Press, 1955, Philosophical Library, New York, 1956

Cockett S.R. and Hilton K.A. *Dyeing of Cellulosic Fibres and Related Processes* Leonard Hill, 1961, Academic Press, New York, 1961

The Colour Index vols i–iv, Society of Dyers and Colourists and the American Association of Textile Chemists and Colorists

Desirens L. *The Chemical Technology of Dyeing and Printing* 2 volumes, Reinhold Publishing Company, New York, 1951

Dumas J.B. *Precis de l'art de la teinture* Paris, 1846 (in French; a most popular work at the time with many contemporary references)

Hall A.J. *A Handbook of Textile Dyeing and Printing* National Trade Press Ltd, London, 1955

Home F. *Experiments on Bleaching* Edinburgh, 1756

Horsfall R.S. and Lawrie L.G. *The Dyeing of Textile Fibres* Chapman and Hall, London, 1949

Hummell J.J. *The Dyeing of Textile Fabrics* Cassell, London, 1890 (summarizes available information with many diagrams of techniques and machinery in use at that time)

Lawrie L.G. *A Bibliography of Dyeing and Textile Printing (1570–1946)* Chapman and Hall, London, 1949

Macquer P.S. *Art de la teinture en soie* France, 1763 (in French, also in English translation of part, 1789 and 1901)

Mallor C.M. and Cardell D.S.L. *Dyes and Dyeing. 1775–1860* British Journal for the History of Science, June 1963

Pellew C.E. *Dyes and Dyeing* Sampson Low, London, 1928 (a most useful study for information up to the twenties)

Le Pileur D'A Pligny *L'art de la teinture des fils et etoffes des ventables causes de la fixite des couleurs de bon teint et suivi des cultures du pastel, de la gaude et de la garance* Paris, 1776 (in French, in English 1789 and 1901)

Singer C. *The Earliest Chemical Industry* London, 1948 (the history of alum)

Trotman E.R. *The Dyeing and Chemical Technology of Textile Fibres* Griffin, London, 3rd edit. 1964

NATURAL DYESTUFFS

Bolton E. *Lichens for Vegetable Dyeing* Studio, London, 1960

CIBA Reviews—Particularly numbers 1, 10, 18, 21, 27, 103, 1961/5

Dye Plants and Dyeing—A handbook Brooklyn Botanic Garden, Brooklyn N.Y., 1964 (full of many unusual facts and recipes)

Hurry. *The Woad Plant and its Dye* London, 1930

Kierstead S.P. *Natural Dyes* Bruce Humphries, Boston, U.S.A., 1950

Mairet E.M. *A Book of Vegetable Dyes* S. Dominics Press, Ditchling, Sussex, England, 1920 (history and practical recipes)

Pope F.W. *Processes in Dyeing with Vegetable Dyes and Other Means* North Bennet Street Industrial School, Mass., U.S.A., 1960

Thurstan V. *The Use of Vegetable Dyes* Dryad Press, Leicester, England, 1957

Young S. *Navajo Native Dyes*. US Dept of Interior, 1940

PRINTED TEXTILES FROM 1750

Bancroft E. *Experimental Researches concerning the Philosophy of Permanent Colours; and the Best Means of Producing them, by Dyeing, Calico Printing, etc.* 2 volumes, London, 1813 (standard work. It can be regarded as a summary of all the available knowledge at this period upon textile dyeing and printing)

Berthollet C.L. *Essay on the new method of bleaching by means of oxygenated muriatic acid . . .* London, 1791; *Élements de l'art de teinture* Paris, 1791 (in French), 1824 (in English)

BLOCK PRINTING AND OTHER TECHNIQUES

(A number of books including the early development of printed fabrics will be found in the final section of these notes)

Erickson E. *Block Printing on Textiles* Watson-Guptill Publications, New York, 1961

CIBA Reviews—Particularly numbers 26, 31, 89, 105 and, for markets and trade in the Middle Ages, numbers 62, 64, 65

ROLLER PRINTING

CIBA Review—Particularly number 125. The subject is also covered in many general books upon textile printing

SCREEN PRINTING

Biegeleisen J.I. *Silk Screen Printing Production* Dover Publications Inc., New York, 1963

Biegeleisen J.I. and Cohn M.A. *Silk Screen Techniques* Dover Publications Inc., New York, 1958

Carr F. *A Guide to Screen Process Printing* Studio Vista Limited, London, 1961

CIBA Review—Particularly number 107. The subject is also covered in many general books upon textile printing

Hiett H.L. and Middleton H.K. *Silk Screen Process Production* Blandford Press, 1960

Kosloff A. *The Art and Craft of Screen Process Printing* The Bruce Publishing Company, New York, 1960

Taussig W. *Screen Printing* Clayton Aniline Co, Manchester, 1950

NOTES AND WORKS OF REFERENCE LISTED BY COUNTRIES (SEE ALSO THE FINAL SECTION ON GENERAL BOOKS)

Great Britain

Baines E. (Jun) *History of the Cotton Manufacture in Great Britain* London, 1836 (a standard work upon the subject)

Bunt O.G.E. and Rose E.A. *Two Centuries of English Chintz 1750–1950* F. Lewis, England, 1957 (a study of the development of chintz as typified by the firm of Stead, McAlpin & Co)

Catalogue of a Loan Exhibition of English Chintz Victoria and Albert Museum, London or H.M.S.O., 1960 (no illustrations, but full of most useful information)

A Century of Sanderson 1860–1960 Arthur Sanderson and Sons Ltd, Berners Street, London W1, 1960 (obtainable from the firm)

CIBA Review—Particularly number 1961/1

Delormois *L'art de faire l'Indienne a l'instar d'Angleterre, et de composer toutes les couleurs, bon tient, propres a l'Indienne* . . . Paris, 1770 (in French, the best of the early books on calico printing)

English Chintz Small Picture Book No.22, Victoria and Albert Museum, London or H.M.S.O., 1955

English Printed Textiles Large Picture Book No 13, Victoria and Albert Museum, London, or H.M.S.O., 1960 (a very well-illustrated monograph)

Entwisle E.A., Lewis F. and Mellor J.H. *A Century of British Fabrics 1850–1950* F. Lewis, England

Floud P. Three articles on the English contribution to early textile printing in the *Journal of the Society of Dyers and Colourists* Bradford, England, 1960

Floud P. and Morris B. Nine articles on English eighteenth-century copper-plate textiles and early nineteenth-century roller prints in *Antiques Magazine* (New York) March 1957–April 1958

Six articles on English woodblock-printed textiles 1790–1810 in *Connoisseur Magazine* October 1957–February 1959

Gibbs Smith C. *The Great Exhibition of 1851—A Commemorative Album* Victoria and Albert Museum, London or H.M.S.O., 1964

Hunton W.G. *English Decorative Textiles* Tiranti, London, 1930

Hurst J.G. *Edmund Potter and Dinting Vale* E. Potter and Co Ltd, Manchester (excellent account of the founding of a textile firm and the times when it occurred)

King D. Textiles and the Origins of Printing in Europe, in *Pantheon, International Zeitschrift für Kunst* vol XX, pp 23–30, Munich, 1962

Lewis F. *English Chintz* F. Lewis, England, 1935

The Liberty Story and *The Renaissance of Merton Abbey* Liberty & Co Ltd, Regent Street, London W1 (obtainable from the firm)

Macleod R. *Charles Rennie Mackintosh* Country Life, London, 1968 (a well-illustrated account of this member of the Art Nouveau movement). *Charles Rennie Mackintosh*: a catalogue of an Exhibition at the Edinburgh Festival, 1968

Morris W. *The Collected Works of William Morris XXII* (three articles on pattern designs on textiles) London, 1910–15

O'Brien C. *The British Manufacturers Companion and Callico Printers Assistant* London, 1792 (a contemporary account)

Thompson P. *The Work of William Morris* Heinemann, London, 1967 (well illustrated on all aspects of his life and work)

Turnbull G. *A History of Calico Printing Industry of Great Britain* Altrincham, 1951 (a most comprehensive standard work)

Watkinson R. *William Morris as Designer* Studio Vista, London, 1967 (of especial value to the textile student)

SOCIAL CONDITIONS IN THE TEXTILE INDUSTRY

CIBA Reviews—Particularly numbers 1962/2 and 1968/1

Mantoux P. *The Industrial Revolution in the Eighteenth Century* Cape, London, 1961 (revised edition; an excellent account is included of the textile industry at the time as well as a most comprehensive bibliography)

Tippett, L.H.C. *A Portrait of the Lancashire Textile Industry* O.U.P

China
CIBA Review—Particularly number 1963/2

France
CIBA Reviews—Particularly numbers 3, 18, 25, 31, 67

Schwartz P.R. *A Century of French Fabrics 1850–1950* F. Lewis, England

Germany
Bindewald E. and Kasper K. *Fairy Fancy on Fabrics* Georg Westermann Verlag, Braunschweig, 1951

Branford C.T. *Bauhaus Weimar 1919–25, Dessau 1925–28*, Boston, 1952

CIBA Reviews—Particularly numbers 83, 103

Gropius W. *Memorandum to Grand Duke of Saxe Weimar* 1914

India
Baker G.P. *Calico Painting and Printing in the East Indies in the 17th and 18th centuries* 2 vols. Edward Arnold, London, 1921 (with a portfolio of 37 colour collotype plates; outstanding)

Brett K.B. An English Source of Indian Design *Journal of Indian Textile History* Volume I, 1955, pp 40/54; A French Source of Indian Chintz Design *Journal of Indian Textile History* Volume II, 1956, pp 43/52; The Flowering Tree in Indian Chintz *Journal of Indian Textile History* Volume III, 1957, pp 45/57, Calico Museum of Textiles, Ahmedabad

Brief Guide to Oriental Painted Dyed and Printed Textiles Brief Guide No 3, Victoria and Albert Museum, H.M.S.O., London, 1950

Buhler A. Patola Influences in South East Asia *Journal of Indian Textile History* Volume IV, 1959, pp 4/46, Calico Museum of Textiles, Ahmedabad

Designs in Indian Textiles ed Mookerjee A., The Indian Institute of Art in Industry, Calcutta, N.D.

Hadaway W.S. *Cotton Paintings and Printing in the Madras Presidency* Madras, 1917 (a full and illustrated account of the techniques)

Jayakar P. The Dyed Fabrics of India Volume 2, No. 1, pp 93/99 Marg—*A Magazine of Architecture and Art Bombay*

Jayakar P. *Indian Printed Textiles* All India Handicrafts Board, N.D.

Jayakar P. A neglected group of Indian Ikat Fabrics *Journal of Indian Textile History* Volume I, 1955, pp 55/65, Calico Museum of Textiles, Ahmedabad

Krishna V. Flowers in Indian Textile Design *Journal of Indian Textile History* Volume VII, 1967, pp 1/20, Calico Museum of Textiles, Ahmedabad

Lewis A.B. *Block Prints from India for Textiles* Field Museum of Natural History, Chicago, 1924 (illustrations of actual prints)

Mehta R.J. *The Handicrafts and Industrial Arts of India* Tarapovevala, Bombay, 1960

Mehta R.N. Bandhas of Ovissa *Journal of Indian Textile History* Volume VI, 1961, pp 62/14, Calico Museum of Textiles, Ahmedabad

Naqui H.K. Dyeing of Cotton Goods in the Mughal Hindustan (1556–1803) *Journal of Indian Textile History* Volume VII, 1967, pp 45/56, Calico Museum of Textiles, Ahmedabad

Osumi T. *Printed Cottons of Asia* Bijutsu Shuppau-She and Charles E. Tuttle Company Rutland, U.S.A., 1963

Schwartz P.R. French Documents on Indian Cotton Painting (1) The Beaulieu Ms. c. 1734 *Journal of Indian Textile History* Volume II, 1956, pp 5/23; (2) New Light on Old Material *Journal of Indian Textile History* Volume III, 1957, pp 15/44; The Roxburgh Account of Indian Cotton Painting *Journal of Indian Textile History* Volume IV, 1959, pp 47/56, Calico Museum of Textiles, Ahmedabad

TRADE IN INDIAN TEXTILES

CIBA Reviews—Particularly numbers 2 and 36.

Geijer A. Some Evidence of Indo-European Commerce in Pre-Mughal Times *Journal of Indian Textile History* Volume I 1955, pp 34/39, Calico Museum of Textiles, Ahmedabad

Irwin J. Indian Textile Trade in the Seventeenth Century (1) Western India *Journal of Indian Textile History* Volume I, 1955, pp 5/33; (2) Coromandel Coast *Journal of Indian Textile History* Volume II, 1956, pp 24/42; (3) Bengal *Journal of Indian Textile History* Volume III, 1957, pp 59/74; (4) Foreign Influences *Journal of Indian Textile History* Volume IV, 1959, pp 57/64, Calico Museum of Textiles, Ahmedabad

Select Bibliography of Indian Textiles *Journal of Indian Textile History* Volume I, 1955, pp 66/76; Volume II, 1956, pp 58/62, Calico Museum of Textiles, Ahmedabad

Japan

CIBA Review—Particularly numbers 43 and 1967/4

Japan Textile Color Design Center *Textile Designs of Japan*; Volume 1 *Designs in Free Style*; Volume 2 *Designs mainly Geometric*; Volume 3 *Designs with Foreign Influence* Osaka, Japan, F. Lewis, England, 1959, 1960, 1961 (outstanding illustrations and text upon the whole field of Japanese textiles)

Yamanobe T. *Textiles* No. 2, Arts and Crafts of Japan, Charles E. Tuttle Company, Rutland, U.S.A., 1957

Scandinavia

Zahle E. *Scandinavian Domestic Design* Methuen, London, 1963 (a well-illustrated account of all kinds of crafts including textiles with lists of practising craftsmen)

Spain

CIBA Review—Particularly number 1963/3

Switzerland

CIBA Reviews—Particularly numbers 55, 62, 79, 105, 119

GENERAL BOOKS UPON THE HISTORY, DESIGN AND TECHNIQUES OF PRINTED TEXTILES

Encyclopaedia Britannica (contains a number of specialist articles classified under the normal topic headings and giving information of a general nature)

Bindewald E. and Kasper K. *Fairy Fancy on Fabrics* Georg Westermann Verlag, Braunschweig, 1951 (a readable and well-illustrated general account of printed textiles)

Birrell V. *The Textile Arts* Harper and Brothers, New York, 1959 (a very comprehensive account of a wide variety of textile crafts)

Capey R. *The Printing of Textiles* Chapman and Hall, London, 1930 (a most interesting book)

Clouzot H. and Morris F. *Painted and Printed Fabrics* Metropolitan Museum of Art, New York, 1927

Conran T. *Printed Textile Design* Studio, London, 1957

Decorative Art issued annually (1943–8 in one volume) and an invaluable source of illustrations of textiles since 1906, Studio, London

Decorative Art in Modern Interiors ed Ella Moody, issued annually and an excellent illustrated review of current design including textiles, Studio Vista, London

Denny G.G. *Fabrics* J.B. Lippincott, Co, Philadelphia, 1962

Design by the Yard, Textile Printing from 800–1956 New York, The Cooper Union Museum, 1956

European Printed Textiles Large Picture Book No 4, Victoria and Albert Museum, H.M.S.O., London, 1949

Glazier *Historic Textile Fabrics* Batsford, London, 1923

Hollen N. and Saddler J. *Textiles* Collier Macmillan, London, 3rd edit. 1968

Howell-Smith *Western Painted, Dyed and Printed Textiles* Victoria and Albert Museum, London, 1934

Hunter S.L. *Decorative Textiles* Philadelphia, 1918

Johnston M.P. and Kaufman G. *Design on Fabrics* Reinhold, New York, /London 1967

Perceval. *The Chintz Book* Heinemann, London, 1923

PRACTICAL HAND BOOKS AND OTHER TECHNIQUES

Crace-Calvert F. *Dyeing and Calico Printing* Simpkin Marshall, London, 1876

Crookes W. *A Practical Hand Book of Dyeing and Calico Printing* Longmans Green, London, 1874

I.C.I. *An Introduction to Textile Printing* (revised edition) Butterworth/I.C.I., London, 1968

Kale D.G. *Principles of Cotton Printing* Ahmedabad, 1957 (history, recipes and actual printed cloth samples)

Knecht E. and Fothergill J.B. *The Principles and Practice of Textile Printing* Charles Griffin, London, 1912 to 1952 (the standard textbook on the subject)

Persoz, J.F. *Traité theoretique et pratique de l'impression des tissus* 4 volumes, Paris, 1848 (in French and one of the last monumental works on textile printing published just before the introduction of coal tar dyestuffs)

Sanson A. *The Printing of Cotton Fabrics* Simpkin Marshall, London, 1877

Thomson R.D. *Records of General Science* Volume 1, London, 1835

BACKGROUND READING

Amaya M. *Art Nouveau* Studio Vista /Dutton, London and New York, 1966

Bauhaus: a catalogue of the exhibition at the Royal Academy of Arts, London, 1968

Braun-Ronsdorf M. *A History of the Handkerchief* F. Lewis, England, 1967

CIBA Review—Particularly number 89 (The Handkerchief)

Dubois M.J. *Curtains and Draperies* Batsford, London, 1967 (an excellently illustrated account of the uses of textiles in interior decoration from the period of the Renaissance to the end of the last century. Although there is little upon printed textiles as such the illustrations, mostly from contemporary sources, show the uses to which textiles were put during the classic ages)

Hillier B. *Art Deco* Studio Vista/Dutton, London and New York, 1968

Naylor G. *The Bauhaus* Studio Vista/Dutton, London and New York, 1968

Pevsner N. *Pioneers of Modern Design from William Morris to Walter Gropius* Penguin Books, 1960 (an outstanding contribution to an understanding of the roots of contemporary design)

Scheigid W. *Crafts of the Weimar Bauhaus* Studio Vista, London, 1967

GENERAL

Review of Textile Progress 1–17, published jointly by the Textile Institute, The Society of Dyers and Colourists and Butterworths

Textile Terms and Definitions The Textile Institute, 10 Blackfriars Street, Manchester 3, 5th edit. 1963

JOURNALS

THE CIBA REVIEW

One of the most useful of all the publications available for the serious student of dyed and printed textiles is the *CIBA Review*, published (in English, German, French and Italian) since May 1936 by CIBA Ltd, Basle, Switzerland, and circulated to libraries, dyehouses and research institutes. Most aspects of textiles have been covered in the nearly two hundred issues to date each dealing with one particular area of textile study.

The publications are not available for purchase, many are now out of print, nor are copies available to the general public from CIBA. Most large lending libraries possess copies for consultation and students are advised to consult their librarian. The Victoria and Albert Museum Library in London has a complete set for study in the library. Many articles contain detailed bibliographies and excellent illustrations.

A List of Principal Contents of CIBA Review

1 Medieval Dyeing
2 India, its Dyers, and its Colour Symbolism
3 Wall-coverings
4 Purple
5 Tapestry
6 Silks of Lyons
7 Scarlet
8 The Dressing of Hides in the Stone Age
9 Dyeing and Tanning in Classical Antiquity
10 Trade Routes and Dye Markets in the Middle Ages
11 The Early History of Silk
12 Weaving and Dyeing in Ancient Egypt and Babylon
13 Guild Emblems and their Significance
14 Cloth-making in Flanders
15 Pile Carpets of the Ancient Orient
16 The Loom
17 Dress Fashions of the Italian Renaissance
18 Great Masters of Dyeing in Eighteenth-Century France
19 The Exchange
20 The Development of the Textile Crafts in Spain

American Dyestuff Reporter Published fortnightly from Easton, Pennsylvania

Craft Horizons Unusually well-illustrated articles upon the textile crafts in America and outside. Published every other month by the American Craftsmen's Council, 44 West 53rd Street, N.Y. 19 N.Y. U.S.A

Handweaver and Craftsman Published quarterly from 220, Fifth Avenue, New York

International Dyer Published fortnightly by the Textile Press, London

Journal of Indian Textile History Published at irregular intervals by the Calico Museum of Textiles, Ahmedabad, India

Journal of the Society of Dyers and Colourists Published monthly, Bradford. Official organ of the professional body

Journal of the Textile Institute Published by the Institute, 10 Blackfriars Street, Manchester 3

Textile Chemist and Colorist Journal of the American Association of Textile Chemists and Colorists, Research Triangle Park, N. Carolina

Textile History As far as I know this is the only journal devoted to the publication of contemporary research into textile history. Published annually by David and Charles, South Devon House, Railway Station, Newton Abbot, Devon

Victoria and Albert Museum Bulletin Published quarterly.

The following periodicals contain articles at frequent intervals upon contemporary textiles:

Abitare (Italy)

Ambassador (G.B.)

American Fabrics Magazine

Art et Decoration (France)

Design (published monthly by the Council of Industrial Design, The Design Centre, Haymarket, London sw1)

Domus (Italy)

Drapery and Fashion Weekly (G.B.)

Fashion and Fabrics (U.S.A.)

Form (Journal of the Swedish Council of Industrial Design)

Graphis (Switzerland, English edition)

Harpers' Bazaar (U.S.A.)

House Beautiful (U.S.A.)

House and Garden (G.B.)

Interior Design (G.B.)

International Textiles (Holland)

Interni (Italy)

Kaunis Koti (Finnish design)

L'Art et la Mode (France)

Mobilia (Denmark; English and other texts)

Moebel (Interior design, Germany; English summaries)

Textiles Suisses (Switzerland)

Textilveredlung (Switzerland)

Vogue (U.S.A. and G.B.)

Frank's Fashion Guide contains a list of world wide fashion magazines. Obtainable from R. D. Franks Ltd., Kent House, Market Place, Oxford Circus, London, w.1

II Museums and centres with collections of textiles

NOTE *Permission to see reserve collections in all museums should be obtained by applying in writing to the keeper of the appropriate department, stating exact details of the facilities required, and the reasons why such study is necessary. This will help the museum staff to plan their work and also to give the most appropriate assistance.*

GREAT BRITAIN—LONDON

The Victoria and Albert Museum, South Kensington, sw7. The finest collections of textiles (in length and costumes) in the British Isles. Particularly the Department of Textiles, where the primary collection in the Textiles Study Rooms contains a representative selection of embroidered, printed and woven textiles. Serious students may study further in the reserve collections which are among the most comprehensive in the world and include such items as the Aurel Stein collection from Khotan. Do not be misled by the Museum's title, exhibits from all periods and countries are available backed by an exceptionally well informed and co-operative staff.

Housed within the V. and A. is the Indian Section (once the Indian Museum) which is a self-contained department containing a superb collection of Indian culture and particularly Indian textiles of all kinds.

The circulation department contains, amongst much art and crafts material, many examples and photographs of contemporary and older textiles which are available on loan to approved establishments.

The British Museum, Great Russell Street, wc1. Outstanding collections of nineteenth-century textiles from West Africa and the Near East. Particularly the Charles Beving collection of West African tie dye and starch resist fabrics in the Ethnographical Department.

Bethnal Green Museum, Cambridge Heath Road, e2. Costumes, Spitalfield silks and other items such as rare dolls' houses, English silver, etc.

Horniman Museum, London Road, Forest Hill, se23. An excellently arranged ethnographical museum of man, his arts, crafts, etc.

William Morris Gallery (and Brangwyn Gift), Lloyd Park, Walthamstow, e17. An interesting collection of Morris's original designs and examples of craftsmanship.

Other London centres with some textiles, particularly woven, and costume

Commonwealth Institute, Kensington High Street, w8
Gunnersbury Park Museum, Gunnersbury Park, w3
Ham House, Petersham, Richmond
Hampton Court Palace, Hampton Court
Osterley Park House, Osterley
Science Museum, Exhibition Road, South Kensington, sw7

OUTSIDE LONDON

BRADFORD   Society of Dyers and Colourists historical collection

MANCHESTER   *Whitworth Art Gallery*, Oxford Road, University of Manchester. A most important and comprehensive collection

MANCHESTER   Collections of English Calico, Printing Division, Oxford Street

OXFORD   *The Pitt Rivers Museum*, Parks Road. An interesting collection of ethnographical material

Other museums outside London with textiles particularly woven, machinery or costume

ARMAGH   *County Museum*, The Mall, Northern Ireland (costume)

BANGOR   *Museum of Welsh Antiquities*, University College of North Wales, College Road (textiles, costume)

BARNARD CASTLE   *The Bowes Museum*, Co. Durham (tapestries, costume)

BASINGSTOKE   *The Willis Museum*, New Street, Hants (costume)

BATH   *American Museum in Britain*, Claverton Manor, Near Bath (costume, textiles)

BATH   *Holburne of Menstrie Museum of Art*, Great Pulteney Street (costume)

BATH   *Museum of Costume, Assembly Rooms* (costume collection founded by Mrs Langley Moore, an outstanding exhibition from the seventeenth century to the present day)

BATLEY   *Bagshaw Museum, Wilton Park* (textile industry bygones, etc.)

BEDFORD   *Cecil Higgins Art Gallery*, Castle Close

BELFAST   *Ulster Museum*, Stranmillis, Northern Ireland (ethnographical material spinning wheels, etc.)

BIRMINGHAM   *City Museum and Art Gallery*, Cingreve Street, 3 (costume, ethnographical material)

BLACKBURN   *'Lewis' Textile Museum*, (spinning and weaving industries and their development)

BLAIR ATHOLL   *Blair Castle and Atholl Museum*, Perthshire, Scotland (costume)

BOLTON   *Hall i'th'wood Museum* (home of Samuel Crompton (1753–1827), inventor of the spinning mule)

BOLTON   *Museum and Art Gallery*, Civic Centre (costume, etc.)

BOLTON   *Tonge Moor Textile Machinery Museum*, Tonge Moor Road (historic textile machinery)

BRADFORD   *Bolling Hall*, Bowling Hall Road (costumes)

BRISTOL   *City Art Gallery*, Queen's Road, 8 (applied art and costume)

BURNLEY   *Gawthorpe Hall* (textiles, embroidery, lace, costumes, etc., library and special student facilities)

CAMBRIDGE   *Fitzwilliam Museum*, Trumpington Street

CHRISTCHURCH   *Red House Museum and Art Gallery*, Quay Road (costumes)

COVENTRY   *Herbert Art Gallery and Museum*, Jordan Well (silk ribbon industry)

DUNDEE   *City Museums and Art Galleries*, Albert Square, Scotland (costume)

EDINBURGH   *Huntly House*, Canongate, 8, Scotland (trade guilds and costume)

EDINBURGH   *Royal Scottish Museum*, Chambers Street, 1, Scotland (costume, textile industry)

EXETER   *Royal Albert Memorial Museum and Art Gallery*, Queen Street (costume, ethnography)

FORFAR   *The Meffan Institute Museum*, Angus, Scotland (costume)

GLASGOW   *Art Gallery and Museum*, Kelvingrove, Scotland (costume, Oriental objects, tapestries, ethnography)

GLASGOW   *Old Glasgow Museum People's Palace*, Scotland (costume)

GLENESK   *Folk Museum*, The Retreat, Angus, Scotland (costume)

GUERNSEY *Hauteville House* (Victor Hugo's House), Hauteville Street, St Peter Port, Channel Islands (tapestries)

GUILDFORD *Museum and Muniment Room*, Castle Arch (needlecrafts)

HALIFAX *Bankfield Museum and Art Gallery*, Akroyd Park (textile machinery, textiles, costume)

HARTLEBURY *Worcestershire County Museum*, Hartlebury Castle, Hartlebury, near Kidderminster (costume, mural crafts)

HAWICK *Wilton Lodge Museum*, The Park, Roxburgh, Scotland (costume, hosiery machinery)

HEREFORD *Churchill Gardens Museum*, Venn's Lane (costume)

HEREFORD *City Museum and Art Gallery*, Broad Street, (costume, textiles)

HUDDERSFIELD *The Tolson Memorial Museum*, Ravensknowle Park, Wakefield Road (costume)

ILKLEY *Manor House Museum and Art Gallery*, Castle Yard (costume)

IPSWICH *Museum*, High Street (costume)

KEIGHLEY *Art Gallery and Museum*, Cliffe Castle (applied arts, craft workshop)

KIRKCALDY *Museum and Art Gallery*, War Memorial Grounds, Scotland

LANCASTER *Museum*, Old Town Hall, Market Square (industries, costume)

LEEDS *Temple Newsam* (costume)

LEEDS *Abbey House Museum*, Kirkstall (folk costume)

LEICESTER *Newarke Houses Museum*, The Newarke (costume)

LEIGH *Pennington Hall Museum and Art Gallery*, Pennington Hall (former silk industry)

LEWES *Anne of Cleves House*, High Street, Southover (costume)

LUTON *Museum and Art Gallery*, Wardown Park (rural trades and crafts including straw hat and pillow lace, costume, needlecraft accessories)

MAIDSTONE *Museum and Art Gallery*, St Faith's Street (costume, etc.)

MANCHESTER *Gallery of English Costume*, Platt Hall, Rusholme (costume from seventeenth century to the present day)

MANCHESTER *Museum of Art and Crafts*, The University, Oxford Road (ethnology)

NEWCASTLE UNDER LYME *Borough Museum and Art Gallery*, Brampton Park (textiles)

NEWCASTLE UPON TYNE *Laing Art Gallery and Museum*, Higham Place (textiles, costume)

NORWICH *Castle Museum* (costume)

NORWICH *Bridewell Museum of Local Industries and Rural Crafts*, Bridewell Alley (local crafts including textiles)

NOTTINGHAM *City Museum and Art Gallery*, The Castle (costume, textiles, lace)

PAISLEY *Museum and Art Galleries*, High Street, Scotland (Paisley shawls: a most comprehensive exhibition including shawls, manufacturers' sample books, designers' sketches, weavers tools, looms, etc)

PORT SUNLIGHT *The Lady Lever Art Gallery*

READING *Museum and Art Gallery*, Blagrave Street

READING *Museum of English Rural Life* (textile crafts)

ST FAGANS *Welsh Folk Museum*, St Fagans Castle, Wales (costume, etc.)

SOUTHAMPTON *Tudor House Museum*, St Michael's Square (costume)

STOKE-ON-TRENT *City Museum and Art Gallery*, Broad Street, Hanley (costume, samplers)

WADDESTON *Waddeston Manor*, Bucks (carpets, tapestries)

WARWICK *St John's House*, Coten End (costume)

YORK *Castle Museum*, Tower Street (outstanding as a Folk Museum. Costumes, early crafts, samplers)

Centres with exhibitions of contemporary textile design

The Bladon Gallery, Hurstbourne Tarrant, Andover, Hants. A society of craftsmen who exhibit and sell in these galleries a wide range of craftwork including textiles

Bluecoat Display Centre, 50 Bluecoat Chambers, School Lane, Liverpool 1.

Crafts Centre of Great Britain, 43 Earlham Street, Covent Garden, London WC2. Exhibitions and sales by craftsmen including textile designers and makers

Crafts Council of Great Britain, 47 Victoria Street, London SW1. An association of craftsmen holding regular exhibitions

Design Centre, 28 Haymarket, London SW1. A permanent but constantly changing exhibition of well-designed modern British goods in current production including printed and woven textiles

The Society of Craftsmen, Old Kemble Galleries, 29 Church Street, Hereford.

The Textile Council (formerly The Cotton Board), 3 Alberton Street, Manchester 3. Changing exhibitions particularly of design as applied to textiles

---

EUROPE

Belgium

TERUUREN *Museum of Textiles*

Czecho-slovakia

BARDEJOV *Šariš Museum*

BRATISLAVA *Slovak Museum*

BRATISLAVA *Centre of Popular Art Production*

BRATISLAVA *Slovak Popular Art Group*

DRŮR KRÁLOVÉ n L *Textile Museum*

KOŠICE *State Museum*

PRAGUE *Folk Lore Museum*

Denmark

COPENHAGEN *Museum of Industrial Art*

Finland

HELSINKI *National Museum*

France

PARIS *Musée de L'Homme*. A most interesting museum with many comprehensive collections covering a wide variety of ethnographical and other material

PARIS *Musée des Arts Decoratifs*

PARIS *Cluny Museum*

PARIS *Gobelins Museum*

LYONS *Musée historique des Tissus*

MULHOUSE, ALSACE *Musée de I'Impression sur Étoffes*. An outstanding and unique collection of printed textiles of all types

ORLÉANS *Museum*

Germany

BERLIN *Staatliche Museum* (formerly)

BERLIN *Kunstgewerbe Museum*
BERLIN *Schloss Museum*
COLOGNE *Kunstgewerbemuseum*
CREFELD (KREFELD) Collection of woven textiles
DRESDEN *Museum für Kunsthandwerk*
LEIPZIG *Museum des Kunsthandwerks*
MUNICH *Kunstgewerke Museum*

Italy
FLORENCE *Museo Nazionale*
GENOA *Palazzo Municipio*
ROME *Museo Preistorico Etnografico 'Luigi Pigorini'*
ROME *Vatican Museo Cristiano*
TURIN *Archaeological Museum*
VENICE *Correr Museum*

Netherlands
AMSTERDAM *Archives Indisch Institut*
AMSTERDAM *Royal Tropical Institute*
BRUSSELS *Cinquantaire Museum*
LEIDEN *Ethnographical Museum*

Poland
CRACOW *Museum*

Russia
LENINGRAD *Hermitage Museum*

Spain
MADRID *Archeological Museum*
TARRASA *Textile Museum*

Sweden
STOCKHOLM *Nordiska Museet*
STOCKHOLM *Statens Historiska Museet*

Switzerland
ASCONA *A. G. Kohler Collection*
BASLE *Museum für Völkerkunde*
BASLE *Musée Ethnographique*
BERNE *Historical Museum*
LAUSANNE *Musée d'Art Decoratif de la Ville de Lausanne*
ZÜRICH *Museum Bellerive*
ZÜRICH *University Ethnographical Collection*
ZÜRICH *A. Steinman Collection*

U.S.A.
NEW YORK *American Museum of Natural History*
NEW YORK *Bertha Schaefer Gallery*
NEW YORK *Brooklyn Museum*
NEW YORK *Cooper Union Museum for the Arts of Decoration*

NEW YORK   *Metropolitan Museum of Art*
NEW YORK   *Museum of the City of New York*
NEW YORK   *Sealamandre Museum of Textiles*
NEW YORK   *Smithsonian Institution*
NEW YORK   *State Historical Association, Cooperstown*
AMHERST   *Amherst College, Mead Art Building, Massachusetts*
BALTIMORE   *Maryland Historical Society*
BEVERLY   *Beverly Historical Society, Massachusetts*
BOSTON   *Isabella Stewart Gardner Museum*
BOSTON   *Museum of Fine Arts, Massachusetts*
BRANSON   *Powersite Museum, Missouri*
CHICAGO   *Art Institute, Illinois*
CLEVELAND   *Museum of Art*
COLUMBUS   *The Museum and Library of the Ohio Historical Society*
DANVERS   *Danvers Historical Society Museum, Massachusetts*
DAVENPORT   *Davenport Public Museum, Iowa*
DEARBORN   *Henry Ford Museum and Greenfield Village, Michigan*
DEERFIELD   *Heritage Foundation, Massachusetts*
DEERFIELD   *Pocumtuck Valley Memorial Association*
DETROIT   *Children's Museum, Detroit Public School*
DETROIT   *Institute of Arts, Michigan*
ELSAH   *School of Nations Museum, Illinois*
FALL RIVER   *Fall River Historical Society, Massachusetts*
FARGO   *Cass City Historical Society Museum, North Dakota*
FITCHBURG   *Fitchburg Historical Society, Massachusetts*
FLINT   *Flint Institute of Arts, Michigan*
GAINESVILLE   *Florida State Museum, University of Florida*
GOLDEN   *Pioneer Museum, Colorado*
HADLEY   *Porter-Phelps-Huntington History Museum, Massachusetts*
HARTFORD   *Wadsworth Atheneum, Connecticut*
HOPEDALE   *Little Red Shop, Massachusetts*
KESHENA   *Angus F. Lookaround Memorial Museum and Studio, Wisconsin*
LANCASTER   *Andrew Jackson Historical State Park, South Carolina*
LOS ANGELES   *County Museum, California*
MARIETTA   *Campus Martius Museum, Ohio*
MEMPHIS   *Brooks Memorial Art Gallery, Tennessee*
MERIDEN   *Meriden Historical Society, Connecticut*
NEVADA   *Nevada Historical Society*
NEWARK   *Newark Museum, New Jersey*
NEW HAVEN   *Yale University, Connecticut*
NORMAN   *J. Willis Stovall Museum of Science and History, University of Oklahoma*
NORTH ANDOVER   *Merrimack Valley Textile Museum, Massachusetts*
NORTH PLATTE   *D.A.R. Museum, Nebraska*
OAKLAND   *Mills College Art Gallery, California*
OWATONNA   *Steele County Historical Society, Minnesota*

PAWTUCKET   *Old Slater Mill Museum, Rhode Island*
PHILADELPHIA   *Drexel Institute of Technology Museum*
PHILADELPHIA   *Museum of Art*
PITTSBURGH   *Carnegie Museum, Carnegie Institute*
RICHMOND   *The Valentine's Museum, Virginia*
ROCK ISLAND   *Augustana College Museum, Illinois*
ST PETERSBURG   *Museum of Fine Arts, Florida*
SALEM   *Essex Institute, Massachusetts*
SAN FRANCISCO   *M. H. de Young Memorial Museum, California*
SHELBURNE   *Shelburne Museum, Vermont*
SOUTH BEND   *The Northern Indiana Historical Society*
SPRINGFIELD   *Springfield Historical Society, New Jersey*
STOCKTON   *San Joaquin Pioneer Museum and Haggin Art Galleries, California*
TERRE HAUTE   *Historical Museum of Wabash Valley, Indiana*
UNIVERSITY PARK   *New Mexico State University Museum*
WASHINGTON D C   *Daughters of the American Revolution Museum*
WASHINGTON D C   *Dumbarton Oaks Research Library and Collection*
WASHINGTON D C   *Smithsonian Institution, Museum of History and Technology*
WASHINGTON   *Textile Museum*
WENHAM   *Wenham Historical Museum and Association, Massachusetts*
WILLIAMSBURG   *Colonial Museum, Virginia*
WINTERTHUR   *Henry Francis de Pont Winterthur Museum, Delaware, Ohio*

Canada
TORONTO   *Royal Ontario Museum*

Hawaii
HONOLULU   *B. P. Bishop Museum*

Peru
LIMA   *Museo Nacional de Antropologia y Arqueologia*

ASIA

India
AHMEDABAD   *Calico Museum of Textiles*
BOMBAY   *Prince of Wales Museum of West Africa*
NEW DELHI   *Crafts Museum*
NEW DELHI   *All India Handicrafts Board*

Japan
OSAKA   *Textile, Color and Design Center*
TOKYO   *National Museum*

AFRICA

Egypt
CAIRO   *Boulak Museum*
CAIRO   *Coptic Museum*
CAIRO   *Museum of Egyptian Antiquities*

III Libraries and booksellers

Libraries with specialist sections dealing with textiles

GREAT BRITAIN

Victoria and Albert Museum, South Kensington, London, sw 7. An exceedingly comprehensive specialist library

British Museum, Great Russell Street, London, wc1

Design Centre, Haymarket, London, sw1

Bradford, Glasgow, Leeds, Manchester Libraries all have good textile collections. In addition one can consult the *Society of Dyers and Colourists*, 194 Piccadilly, Bradford, Yorks. The *Textile Institute*, 10 Blackfriars Street, Manchester, 3, provides information for its members.

Burnley, Bawthorpe Hall has a library and student facilities for the study of textiles.

U.S.A.

Textile Design

MASSACHUSETTS

Museum of Fine Arts Library. Huntington Avenue, 479, Boston

Lowell Technological Institute, Alumni Memorial Library. Textile Avenue, Lowell

NEW YORK

Brooklyn Museum, Art Reference Library. Eastern Parkway, Brooklyn 11201

The Cooper Union for the Advancement of Science and Art, Museum Library. Cooper Square, New York City

Metropolitan Museum of Art, Costume Institute, Costume Reference Library. Fifth Avenue at 82nd Street, New York City 10028

New York Public Library, Art and Architecture Division. Fifth Avenue at 42nd Street, New York City 10018

Syracuse University Libraries, Art Library. Room 203, Carnegie Library, Syracuse, New York 13210.

NORTH CAROLINA

Public Library of Charlotte and Mecklenburg County. 310 North Tryon Street, Charlotte 28202

OHIO

Cleveland Institute of Art Library. 11141 East Boulevard, Cleveland

RHODE ISLAND

Rhode Island School of Design Library. 2 College Street, Providence

Textile Industry and Fabrics

ALASKA

Auburn University Library. Auburn
West Point Manufacturing Co. Research Division Library. Shawmut

COLORADO

Gates Rubber Co, Technical Department Library. 999 South Broadway, Denver

DISTRICT OF COLUMBIA

Textile Museum Library. 2320 South Street, North-west Washington 20008

FLORIDA

The Chemstrand Corp, Technical Library. 421 Semur Road, Pensacola

GEORGIA

Georgia Institute of Technology, Price Gilbert Memorial Library. 225 North Avenue, North-West Atlanta
Gallaway Mills Co, Research and Development Division Library. La Grange

ILLINOIS

Sears, Roebuck and Co, Merchandise Testing and Development Laboratory Library. 925 Homan Avenue, Chicago

MASSACHUSETTS

Massachusetts State Department of Commerce Library. 150 Causeway Street, Boston
Museum of Fine Arts. Boston, Massachusetts 02115
Massachusetts Institute of Technology Engineering Library. Cambridge, Mass. 02139
Lowell Technological Institute, Alumni Memorial Library. Textile Avenue, Lowell
Merrimack Valley Textile Museum Library. Massachusetts Avenue, North Andover, Massachusetts 01845
Southeastern Massachusetts Technological Institute Library. North Dartmouth, Mass. 02747
Old Sturbridge Village Library. Sturbridge Massachusetts 01566
Whitin Machine Works Technical Library. Whitinsville, Massachusetts

NEW JERSEY

American Cyanamid Co, Research Division, Bound Brook Laboratories Library. Bound Brook
Nopco Chemical Co, Inc. Library. First and Essex Streets, Harrison
Textile Research Institute Library. Kingston Road, Princeton

NEW MEXICO

Library of Museum of International Folk Art. Museum of New Mexico, P.O. Box 2087, Santa Fe 87501

NEW YORK

Ellington and Co, Inc. Library. 535 Fifth Avenue, New York City
Fairchild Publications, Inc, Costume Library. 7 East 12th Street, New York City
Fashion Institute of Technology. 227 West 27th Street, New York City 10001
Interchemical Corporation. Central Research Laboratories Library. 432 West 45th Street, NYC
Museum of Modern Art Library. 11 West 53rd Street, New York 19
National Federation of Textiles Library. 389 Fifth Avenue, New York City
New York Public Library, Science and Technology Division. Fifth Avenue and 42nd Street, New York City 10018
Scudder, Stevens and Clark Library. 300 Park Avenue, New York City

NORTH CAROLINA

Public Library of Charlotte and Mecklenburg County. 310 North Tryon Street, Charlotte 28202
Gaston County Library. Gastonia
North Carolina State University, D.H. Hill Library. Raleigh, North Carolina 27607

OHIO

Midland Ross Corporation, IRC Fibers Division Library. Mary C. Dilorio, Libn. P.O. Box 580, Painseville 44077

OREGON

Oregon State College Library. Corvallis

PENNSYLVANIA

Millersville State Teachers College Library, Marguerite Porter Davison Collection. Millersville
E. F. Houghton Co. Library. 303 West Lehigh Avenue, Philadelphia
Philadelphia Textile Institute, Hesslein Library. 3243 School House Lane, Philadelphia
Pennsylvania State University, Home Economics Library. Room 10, Home Economics Bldg, University Park, Pa. 16802

RHODE ISLAND

Old Slater Mill Museum. P.O. Box 727, Roosevelt Avenue, Pawtucket
Providence Public Library. 150 Empire Street, Providence, Rhode Island 02903

SOUTH CAROLINA

Greenville County Library. 420 North Main Street, Greenville 29601
Deering Milliken Research Corporation Library. Box 1927, Spartanburg, S.C. 29301

TENNESSEE

National Cotton Council of America Library. P.O. Box 9905, Memphis

VIRGINIA

Institute of Textile Technology Library. Charlottesville 22902

E.I. du Pont de Nemours and Co, Inc, Benger Laboratory Library, Textile Fibers Department, Waynesboro

The Dow Chemical Co. Library. James River Division, Williamsburg, Virginia 23185

Textile Industry and Fabrics—History

Textile Museum Library. 2320 South Street, North West Washington, D.C.

Boston Public Library. Cur. of Engineering Sciences. Copley Square Boston, Mass. 02117

Old Sturbridge Village Library. Sturbridge, Massachusetts 01566

Providence Public Library. Textile Collection. 150 Empire Street, Providence, Rhode Island 02903

Textiles, Ancient

Textile Museum Library. 2320 South Street, N.W. Washington, D.C. 20008

CANADA

Ontario Research Foundation Library. 43 Queen's Park, Toronto 5, Ontario

Dominion Textile Co. Limited. 1950 Sherbrooke St. W, Montreal, Quebec

Booksellers specializing in crafts and particularly textiles

GREAT BRITAIN

K.R. Drummond, 30 Hart Grove, Ealing Common, London, w5, is the only specialist shop as far as I know who, although stocking, obtaining and selling all new and second-hand books on Arts and Crafts in their widest sense, also specializes in Textiles and produces admirable catalogues.

F. Lewis, Publishers Ltd, The Tithe House, 1461 London Road, Leigh-on-Sea, England. An outstanding publisher of books on textiles and other art subjects. Many excellent series, including *A Survey of World Textiles* (one volume per country). They are also official representatives of many foreign specialist publishers.

Booksellers with substantial stocks dealing with textiles

GREAT BRITAIN

Foyles Bookshop, Charing Cross Road, London

T.N. Lawrence and Son Ltd, 2–4 Bleeding Heart Yard, London, EC1

London Art Bookshop (Tirantis), 72 Charlotte Street, London, W1

Messrs Luzac of Great Russell Street, London (Indian and Far East textiles)

Textile Institute, 10 Blackfriars Street, Manchester 3

Victoria and Albert Museum, South Kensington, London, sw7 (or HM Stationery Offices). A variety of handbooks on such topics as William Morris, Embroidery, Printed Textiles, etc.

Zwemmers Bookshop, Charing Cross Road, London

U.S.A.

Creative Hands Bookshop, Printers Building, Worcester, Mass, U.S.A.

Perkins Oriental Books, 255 Seventh Avenue, New York

Charles E. Tuttle Co., Rutland, Vermont and Tokyo, Japan

IV Educational aids

Illustrations

The British Museum, Victoria and Albert Museum, The Design Centre, together with most other Museums will supply black and white photographs to order at varying prices (depending upon size) of the items in their collections. Usually exhibits may be photographed by visitors and by previous arrangement with the museum concerned. Coloured transparencies and copy transparencies are also often available.

The Miniature Gallery, 60 Rushett Close, Long Ditton, Surrey, supply many sets and single transparencies of an exceedingly high standard of all types of textiles. They issue very full catalogues and are agents in this country for transparencies prepared by Dr Block of Hollywood, California. These cover many crafts, both historic and contemporary and include a large number of textiles.

All the following firms produce filmstrips and/or transparencies, some of which are of textiles.

Educational Productions Ltd, 17 Denbigh Street, London SW1
Visual Publications Ltd, 197 Kensington High Street, London W8
Diana Wyllie Ltd, London
Pictorial Colour Slides, 242 Langley Way, West Wickham, Kent
The Education Division, G.B. Instructional Ltd, Imperial House, 80–82 Regent Street, London W1
Looking and Seeing Filmstrips, 81 Southway, London N20

U.S.A.

Dr Block Color Productions, 1309 North Genesee Avenue, Hollywood 46, California, publishes some of the finest textile transparencies available.

GENERAL

Bossert, Th. *Folk Art of Primitive Peoples, Folk Art of Europe* and *Decorative Art of Egypt*, Zwemmer, London. These invaluable books contain many hundreds of illustrations, mostly in colour, of all types of crafts, including textiles. Explanatory notes are also included.

Samples and leaflets

These can be obtained at a reasonable price from a large number of firms and organizations, including

British Man-Made Fibres Federation,
Bridgewater House, 58 Whitworth Street, Manchester 1
British Wool Marketing Board,
Kew Bridge House, Kew Bridge Road, Brentford, Middlesex
The Textile Council (formerly the Cotton Board),
3 Alberton Street, Manchester 3

Design Centre,
28 Haymarket, London SW1

The Flaxspinners and Manufacturers' Association of Great Britain,
Public Relations Officer, 4 Chamber of Commerce Buildings, Dundee

The Silk Centre,
Dorland House, 18–20 Regent Street, London SW1

Illustrated pamphlets and booklets upon a wide variety of textiles are published by the Victoria and Albert Museum in particular.

Actual samples of textiles may often be purchased from The Folio Society, 6 Stratford Place, London W1.

Eaton Bag Company, Manette Street, London (between Foyles' Bookshops), sells original, contemporary printed tapa or bark cloth from the South Seas.

Lullingstone Silk Farm, Ayot House, Ayot St. Lawrence, Herts—the only silk farm in the country where visitors, including school parties, may see all the stages of silk production.

Courses for textile printers

There are many courses and summer schools held throughout the country by local education authorities and private bodies that offer classes or groups in varying textile techniques. It is becoming increasingly difficult to find practical courses in colleges of art for the home craftsmen or teacher not wishing to take a diploma course.

We would recommend the following:

GREAT BRITAIN

(1) The excellent practical courses at Dartington conducted by Susan Bosence and Annette Kok, upon dyeing and printing techniques (including batik, tie and dye, natural dyes, etc.) which take place during vacations. For details of these and others held by various Guilds of Craftsmen write to the Warden, Devon Centre for Further Education, Dartington College of Arts, Totnes, Devon (Totnes 2267).

(2) The annual summer school held by the Association of Guilds of Weavers, Spinners and Dyers at different places in England and the regular meetings held by the many regional guilds of this Association. The honorary secretary, Miss Mary Blair, Greengate, Taporley, Cheshire, will supply full details and the address of your nearest guild secretary.

(3) The annual Cardiff summer schools (Cardiff Education Authority for details) has extensive sections upon decorative textile constructions and other techniques.

U.S.A.

Craft Horizons issued every other month by the American Craftsmen's Council, 16 East 52nd Street, New York, N.Y., carries regular supplements with details of courses and schools held throughout the States. It also issues an annual Crafts Courses Directory obtainable from Publications Department, A.C.C. 29 West 53rd Street, N.Y., N.Y. 10019.

Index

ACKNOWLEDGEMENTS

The author and publishers would like to thank the following museums, private individuals and other establishments for their kindness in allowing works in their possession to be illustrated in this book: Ascher (London) Ltd—No. 69; Trustees of the British Museum—No. 14; Conran Fabrics—Nos 73, 76; Coventry College of Education—Nos 67, 74, 79, 80, 81, 84, 85; Edinburgh Weavers—No. 72; M. Feldman Esq—No. 7; Heal Fabrics Ltd —Nos 51, 70, 71; Historical Museum, Basle—No. 10; Hull Traders—No. 77; Manchester City Art Galleries —Nos 21, 22; James Meldrum Esq—No. 59; Musée de l'Impression sur Etoffes, Mulhouse—Nos 26, 32; Philadelphia Museum of Art—No. 18; J. G. Roth Esq —Nos 17, 19, 28, 29, 30; Royal College of Art—No. 53; Sanderson Fabrics— Nos 52, 78, 82, 87, 88, 89, 90; H. Steiner, Esq—No. 86; Trondheim Museum, Norway—Nos 57, 58, and the Victoria and Albert Museum—Nos 5, 6, 8, 9, 11, 20, 24, 25, 31, 33, 34, 35, 38, 39, 41, 42, 44, 45–50, 54, 55, 56, 60–66, 68. Thanks are also due to the *CIBA Review* for permission to reproduce Nos 1, 2, 3, 4, 10, 12, 13, 15, 16, 18, 26, 32, 33, 36, 40, 41, 42, and *Design Magazine*—No. 53. David Bailey—No. 75; Forrer—Nos 1, 2, 3, 4; Helmut Newton—No. 83; J. P. Schwartz—Nos 26, 32; Muriel Somerfield—Nos 24, 27, 34, 35, 43, 44, 50, and Tim Street-Porter—No. 53, were responsible for taking the photographs as indicated.